CONTENTED COWS
MOOVE FASTER

HOW GOOD LEADERS GET PEOPLE TO PUT MORE OOMPH! INTO THEIR WORK

BILL CATLETTE & RICHARD HADDEN

R. Brent and Company
Asheville, North Carolina
rbrent.com

Published in Asheville, North Carolina
by R. Brent and Company
P.O. Box 7055
Asheville, NC 28802-7055
828-350-9898
rbrent.com

Editor and publisher: *Robbin Brent Whittington*
Chief editor: *Libby Riker*
Cover design: *Electronic Publishing Services, Inc.*
Cover technical assistance: *io design & illustration, Asheville, North Carolina*
Interior design: *jb graphics, Asheville, North Carolina*
Illustrations and typography: *jb graphics, Asheville, North Carolina*
Compositor: *Electronic Publishing Services, Inc., Jonesborough, Tennessee*

Library of Congress Data

Catlette, Bill and Hadden, Richard.
   contented cows moove faster: how good leaders get people
   to put more oomph! into their work—1st ed.
      p. cm.
   ISBN-13: 978-0-9788160-4-9
   ISBN-10: 0-9788160-4-8
   1. Business Leadership 2. Business Management
   I. Title
First Edition   2007927550 LCCN

14 13 12 11 10 09 08 07   1 2 3 4 5

Printed in the United States of America

To order books, visit: contentedcows.com; e-mail: sales@contentedcows.com, or call:
904.720.0870 for more information.

DEDICATION

Dedicated to Louie Hadden (Richard's dad)
and Mary Catlette (Bill's mom).
They taught us our earliest and most important lessons about
things like honesty, humility, and doing what's right.
We lost them both on the same day, and miss them deeply.

CONTENTS

ACKNOWLEDGEMENTS

This book was an ongoing project for better than three years. We've kidded each other (only half in jest), and been gently reminded by a few people (spouses included), that if more of our own discretionary effort had gone into the project, perhaps it would have been finished sooner. Guilty as charged.

The book is a lot bigger, and better, than the two of us, though. In the course of researching, writing, and publishing it, we benefited from the efforts of many people. Here are just a few of those without whose help we couldn't, and wouldn't have wanted to do it.

The folks at R. Brent and Company. After partnering with us on our first work, publisher Robbin Brent Whittington was brave enough to sign on for a second tour of duty. We appreciate not only the talent she brought to the table, but more important, her attitude and determination to get this thing done well, and on time. Jane Ware and Rick Soldin are responsible for a killer cover and an interior design that makes this a much more pleasant read. Chief editor Libby Riker contributed her considerable editing expertise, working long days, weekends, and holidays on behalf of readers who deserve a well-written book.

Bernie Aller, Beth Irvine, Julie Ladet-Baiardi, and Wayne Reed, who were kind enough to read the manuscript, and courageous enough to tell us what they really thought.

Corporate chieftains Terry Andrus (East Alabama Medical Center), Todd Bruhn (24 Hour Fitness), Dan Cathy (Chick-fil-A), Tim Kern (Pfizer), Diane Raines (Baptist Health Systems), Kathy Rockel and Bob Harvey (Transcription Relief Services), Susan Merfeld and Bill Perocchi (Pebble Beach Company), Steve Swasey (Netflix), and Patrick Lynch (Wegman's Supermarkets), who supported our effort with their ideas, time, and access to their organizations. They contributed mightily to our understanding of this thing called discretionary effort.

ACKNOWLEDGEMENTS

Individuals who, according to their peers and others who know them well, exemplify discretionary effort by going all out every day. We call them "Extra Milers." People such as Command Sgt. Maj. Michele Jones (U.S. Army Reserve), Sgt. 1st Class Jim Lusk (U.S. Army), Eugene Benjamin, M.D. and Hubert Allen (Pebble Beach Company), Kervin Sweet (Chick-fil-A), Lorrie Green (Baptist Medical Center), Verna Crutcher (Delta Air Lines), and Nick Mendez (24 Hour Fitness).

For sharing information about their experiences or organizations, we thank Michael O'Donnell (world-class mountaineer), Jim Catlette (teacher, Langley High School, and brother *par excellence*), Officer Julie Welch (Police Department, Holly Springs, Georgia), Jeromy Williams (Chick-fil-A), Nancy Holland (Erlanger Hospital, Chattanooga, Tennessee), and so many others we've met in our travels.

Since their support of our first work in 1998, we have publicly thanked the folks at Nestle in every speech and seminar for having the good heart to say yes to our request to use the expression "Contented Cows." We remain indebted to them.

Betty Cottle Hadden and Kristi Shea, who continue to do a lot of the important behind-the-scenes stuff that allows us to show up prepared, at the right place, on time, and looking a lot smarter than we really are.

And to our families, who continue to bless us with their love and support.

PREFACE

In December of 1995, we got together in the Delta Crown Room Club at the Orlando International Airport to discuss a book idea that had been rattling around in Bill's head since his early days at FedEx. The two of us had met several years prior, over a broken foot (if we ever have the opportunity to meet you, ask us to expound), and although we were each enjoying working independently, the idea of a partnership was intriguing.

Bill's initial research gave support to the hypothesis that there might be a connection between an organization's leadership and employment practices and its bottom line. After some spirited discussion, we agreed to join forces in exploring the concept further, and to co-author a book that made the business case for treating employees well. Three hours later we broke up the meeting and returned to our respective homes with a pretty solid plan for our first book, *Contented Cows Give Better Milk: The Plain Truth About Employee Relations and Your Bottom Line*, first published in 1998.

In book publishing, as in most other endeavors, timing is, as they say, everything. In this case, it worked both for and against us. The introduction of *Cows I* coincided almost precisely with the turbo-speed growth of the Internet and the popularity of online booksellers such as Amazon.com. Production of the actual printed product was frustrated by a massive diversion of worldwide printing resources for a little book about a boy wizard written at J. K. Rowling's kitchen table in Edinburgh. Moreover, our efforts to secure airtime and ink were overshadowed by the public's insatiable interest in what some called a "minor indiscretion" between a president and a White House intern.

Nevertheless, the word got out. There was a new book out there with a goofy-looking cover, by a couple of unknowns, that made the case—using facts, not faith—that companies that treat their employees well tend to make more money than those that don't. Contented cows give better milk.

We were interviewed by practically every five thousand-watt radio station between Bangor and Burbank. We told our story to business writers from Brussels to Bellingham. A few people even saw us on CNN, MSNBC, Fox News, and Bloomberg. We did book signings at chains and independent book stores across America. Most, except for the one in Richard's parents' neighborhood, were pretty lonely affairs. We sent free books to clients, friends, and former employers, all as part of our grassroots marketing campaign—a campaign that worked remarkably well. Against some pretty long odds, we managed to gain a fair amount of traction. More important, we learned a lot, and really had fun with it.

People talk about a "speaking circuit." No such circuit exists. But many who had read the book were kind enough to ask us to speak and provide leadership training for their association conferences and corporate management meetings. One engagement led to another, both in the U.S. and across the globe. Today, much of our time is devoted to speaking to and consulting with management audiences about how to develop a focused, fired-up, capably led workforce.

After a few years, the inevitable question began to pop up: "So, when's your next book coming out?" Many encouraged us to produce a sequel, *Contented Cows Part Two,* or something similarly titled. We resisted. The business case had already been made, and re-made in a follow-up study that we released in 2002. In fact, every new piece of research we conducted only served to make the original case more compelling.

What we wanted to do then, and have attempted in this volume, is to plumb the depths of one topic we touched on briefly in the original *Cows*—the topic of discretionary effort, that increment of human effort that originates and remains under the control of each individual worker. That morsel of labor that dwells in the gap between what's required of us and what we're capable of.

We knew that discretionary effort—this idea of going above and beyond, or the extra mile—was a critical factor in organizational success. Those who were able to get more effort and engagement, willingly, from more of their people more of the time got better results. But we wanted to know more. Specifically:

- What *is* discretionary effort, really?
- What *good* is it?
- How do you *get* it?

What follows is a comprehensive look at the answers to these questions. We'll define and rename discretionary effort, explore its many benefits, and spend the bulk of the narrative on what you as a leader can do to coax more of it from the people you lead.

This book maintains one feature that was popular among readers of our first work, and introduces another that we hope will be equally helpful. The summaries at the end of each chapter provide the kernels of each chapter's content, in list form. Additionally, we've included for each chapter a section we call "Monday Morning 8 AM"—clear, executable prescriptions for getting more discretionary effort from the people you work with. We suggest you tackle one chapter's worth of these "doable things" at the beginning of each workweek, before you get bogged down with the necessary, the important, the urgent, and the mundane.

Enough of this introductory stuff. Let's get MOOving!

SECTION ONE

OOMPH! MATTERS

1

BALLS TO THE WALL

I firmly believe that any man's finest hour is that moment when he has worked his heart out in a good cause and lies exhausted on the field of battle, victorious. —Vince Lombardi

During the 2001 National Football League season, then-Minnesota Vikings star wide receiver Randy Moss was quoted as saying, "I play when I want to play. Do I play up to my top performance, my ability every time? Maybe not. I just keep doing what I do and that is playing football. When I make my mind up, I am going out there to tear somebody's head off. When I go out there and play football, man, it's not anybody telling me to play or how I should play. I play when I want to play, case closed." Though Moss can be fairly accused of displaying some extremely questionable judgment at times, he clearly understands the implications of his effort, or lack thereof. "With me playing at my highest level, it gives us a better chance to win," he said.[1]

Coming from one of the most gifted players in all of professional sports, Moss's comments struck a nerve with a lot of people, and not just football fans. After all, how dare someone with that much talent, making that much money, give anything less than 100 percent during every play of every practice, let alone every game? Googling the expression "Randy Moss + effort" yields over 100,000 Web page hits, many of which contain a healthy dose of vitriol directed at a guy who, when push came to shove, simply 'fessed up to something that most of us are guilty of on a daily basis: operating on cruise control; playing at something less than our own "A" game potential.

There. It's on the table. Studies have repeatedly shown that most of us operate nowhere near our potential. A survey we conducted of 158 managers and professionals representing a wide spectrum of organizations in both the public and private sectors suggests that most people routinely expend only about 62 percent of their physical, mental, and emotional capacity while at work. Everyone's entitled to a bad day now and then, but that's like taking Thursday afternoon and all day Friday off, every week! It's not that we don't come home tired—far from it. But we're just not operating on all cylinders very often.

When asked how much of their capacity they thought most people routinely expend on non-work activities (hobbies, sports, volunteer, family, etc.), the same respondent group pegged the "ole effort meter" a little higher, at about 75 percent power. See—we can use it when we *want* to. By their own admission, 41 percent of the respondents indicated that they "could contribute substantially more at work, if they wanted to"—emphasis on the last four words. Calling to mind my performance with the last few "honey-do" chores I attempted around the house, I suspect this phenomenon isn't confined to the workplace.

As a case in point, not long ago I* promised my wife that I would install some new blinds in the kitchen on a given weekend. It happened to be the weekend of the NFL Division Championship playoff games. Though I could have awakened early on Saturday and gotten the job done, I didn't, waiting instead until Sunday evening when the games were over and dinner had been concluded.

Moving at barely the minimum posted speed, I trudged to the workroom for tools and then spent nearly an hour reading and rereading the directions. (Why can't they put those things in plain English, with drawings that look a little less like hieroglyphics?) The blinds eventually got hung, and in a reasonably workmanlike manner, but only after I enlisted the aid of our grown daughter to help measure, check levels, and fetch a couple of the necessary adult beverages. Upon relatively objective reflection, I've concluded that, in this particular case, the intensity of effort was scaled back due to one or more of the following factors:

---

*Assuming the reader to be indifferent as to which author is telling a particular story in the first person, we will generally refrain from identifying the narrator of the story. Suffice it to say that both authors agree on the point being illustrated. For those who really want to know, a good rule of thumb is that those stories containing swear words are most likely Bill's.

1. I didn't especially want to have blinds in the kitchen in the first place. Moreover, these blinds were ugly. My commitment to the mission was zilch point two.
2. The task itself was not something I particularly relished. Getting reacquainted with the pooper scooper in the back yard (we have a four-legged burglar alarm) would have been more fulfilling.
3. I was (and still am) fairly certain that, with the blinds hung, one of the next sounds I would hear would have something to do with how nice it would be if we were to repaint the kitchen, as if there ever were a "we" painting project. In other words, performance could prove to be punishing.

As the nature of work has evolved, playing your "C" game is much less conspicuous. No longer do you have to visibly let every third widget go past you on the assembly line in order to withhold discretionary effort. You certainly needn't stage a Christmas day "sick-out" like a number of US Airways flight attendants and baggage handlers did during the 2004 holidays. Instead, for many of us, it's as simple as snoozing through a meeting (with your eyes open, of course), or slowly doing whatever people do in front of a computer monitor all day. Operating on cruise control knows no occupational or hierarchical boundaries. Accountants do it, bankers do it, salespeople do it, school teachers do it, even neurosurgeons do it.

WHAT'S THIS THING CALLED OOMPH!?

Since Elton Mayo's first studies of the relationship between motivation and productivity at the Hawthorne Works of the Western Electric Company in the late 1920s, we've known that each of us has a personal throttle lever by which we regulate the amount of effort we expend on a given activity. We use it when it suits us and the cause seems worthwhile, and withhold it when it doesn't. For that reason, the term came to be known as "discretionary effort." We call it Oomph!

This "throttle lever" provided the basis for our titling of this chapter. (Contrary to what some overly prudish folks may think, it has nothing to do with the male anatomy.) On many early airplanes, the handles or levers controlling the throttle and the fuel mixture were topped with ball-shaped grips, referred to by pilots as (get this) "balls." Pushing the balls forward, toward the front wall of the cockpit (the firewall) resulted in the highest and richest fuel flow to the engines, and the greatest possible speed. In more pedestrian terms, it is akin to "putting the pedal to the metal." So there!

Discretionary effort, or Oomph!, is the level of effort people can give *if they want to.* As it is beyond what is minimally required, there is no penalty for *not* doing it. It cannot be forced. Its expenditure is purely at the discretion of the individual, a decision based more on attitude than fear, necessity, or economic forces. It's what we commonly call going "the extra mile," or "above and beyond the call of duty." We have come to believe that, in nearly all cases, the expenditure of discretionary effort is a conscious, purposeful event. We're deliberately kicking into overdrive. It's not something that happens naturally.

> *The expenditure of discretionary effort is a conscious, purposeful event. We're deliberately kicking into overdrive. It's not something that happens naturally.*

DOWN 'N DIRTY

Oomph! . . . What's It Look Like?

- It's Oomph! when you set the alarm an hour early because you can't wait to get started.
- Oomph! is when, after finishing your assigned part, you readily pitch in to help others.
- Oomph! is when you view assigned goals or quotas as a *minimum* standard.
- When you are Oomphing, time flies. You prefer not to stop for breaks.*
- Oomph! is when you do things that need to be done on your own initiative, rather than because you were asked to.
- Oomph! is making extra effort to satisfy a customer or help a teammate.
- Work is contractual . . . effort is personal.
- Oomphing is fun—really!

*Note to Department of Labor: Oomph! is the complete opposite of involuntary servitude. Leave it alone!

WHAT'S *NOT* OOMPH!?

If Oomph! describes the expenditure of discretionary effort, we'll use the term "ugh" to refer to the lack thereof. Ugh is fine; ugh is OK if good enough is good enough. In stark contrast to Oomph!, ugh represents the minimum level of human effort that is required, or perhaps tolerated, to give the appearance of getting the job done.

> *Work is contractual . . . effort is personal.*

You've seen ugh when the disaffected teenager takes your fast-food order, and does nothing so well as convince you that he or she wants to be anywhere but at work right now. You've heard ugh when the call center worker rattles off some rote and uncaring response to your legitimate complaint about your cable bill. And perhaps you are working in a sea of ugh right now, in a cubicle farm where people are completely uninspired by Dilbertian managers.

> *The Oompher is running to something while typically the workaholic is running away.*

By ugh, we don't mean poor, substandard performance, but everyday, run-of-the-mill effort. People performing as though they were on "cruise control." Nothing special. Nothing inspired. And nothing that stands up very well to good competition. Ugh is just that. Ugh. Ugh will never be able to compete with Oomph!

Oh. And another thing. By Oomph!, we are not—repeat, *not*—talking about being a workaholic. When they are Oomphing, people can put in some incredibly long hours, but the motivation behind the effort is completely different. The Oompher is running *to* something while typically the workaholic is running *away* from some other aspect of their life. "It's not about long hours," says Dr. Bryan Robinson, an Asheville, North Carolina, psychotherapist and author of *Chained to the Desk: A Guidebook for Workaholics, Their Partners and Children, and the Clinicians Who Treat Them.* "It's about the inability to turn it off. It's a question of balance."[2]

WHAT'S SO GREAT ABOUT OOMPH!?

OK, so who cares? What difference does it make whether your people are working with Oomph! or ugh, as long as the unit gets manufactured, the project completed, the meal served, the bed made, or the product sold?

The answer is that it makes a *lot* of difference, especially if things like quality, efficiency, and profit have value in your organization. Our first book, *Contented Cows Give Better Milk*, is chock-full of cold, hard evidence that companies that are great places to work grow faster and make more money.

The difference between Oomph! and ugh is like the difference between Commitment and compliance. When conducting leadership workshops, we frequently get into a discussion with the participant group about the distinction between these two states of mind and approach to work: *Commitment* and *compliance.*

Oomph!
. . . or ugh . . .
inevitably winds up in
the customer's lap.

"Do you want your people Committed—with a capital 'C'—to your organization, your customers, and their jobs?" we'll ask. "Or, given the extra skill and attention required to inspire Commitment, could you settle for compliance, as long as the job gets done?" The usual response is that Commitment is clearly preferable to compliance, probably because Commitment sounds better—loftier. Well, it doesn't just *sound* better. Oomph! embodied by Commitment, is akin to growing a garden in a lush, fertile valley, as opposed to a desert (ugh). The outcome is vastly different.

In the world of business, one reason Oomph! is so important—so absolutely critical to an organization's success—is that Oomph! . . . or ugh . . . inevitably winds up in the customer's lap, one way or the other.

"SECOND MILE SERVICE" AT CHICK-FIL-A

Chick-fil-A, the Atlanta-based quick-service restaurant specializing in chicken sandwiches, waffle fries, and coleslaw, claims in their advertising that they didn't invent the chicken . . . just the chicken sandwich. They may also have invented a culture, for both their customers and their employees, that is virtually unmatched among their fast-food peers. Fresh-ground pepper with your $3 salad. Team members who are encouraged to take the trays to the tables of guests who need a little help, and to place napkins in customers' laps as they're seated.

At Chick-fil-A, the employee's response to a customer's "Thank you" is "My pleasure," not the standard "No problem" that seems to be the reflex of choice among most people in the service sector today. It's all part of what the chain's president and chief operating officer, Dan Cathy, elder son of founder Truett Cathy, calls "Second Mile Service."

Second Mile Service sounds a lot like discretionary effort to us. Oomph! Going above and beyond what's expected to distinguish the customer's experience at Chick-fil-A from . . . you name the competitor. While city-hopping with Dan on the company's time-shared corporate jet (in true Chick-fil-A fashion, a modest Cessna Citation, co-piloted by Dan himself), we had a unique opportunity to observe Chick-fil-A's culture in action, from the top, and to see some of what inspires its people to go the second mile on the job, to give their customers that hard-to-match fast-food experience.

Although Dan is the world's second most ardent cheerleader for the food they serve (Truett's number one), he knows it's not the food that *really* sets them apart. He knows that customers have a tremendous number of choices in what and where they eat, and he believes that Second Mile Service is their best sustainable competitive advantage. "But Second Mile Service doesn't happen in front of the counter unless it first happens behind the counter," Dan told an auditorium partially filled with new Chick-fil-A team members assembled at Des Moines's impressive Science Center of Iowa two days before the opening of the city's first Chick-fil-A. What were fast-food trainees doing at the Science Center of Iowa? Chicken sandwiches can't be that complicated.

They were there as part of the ritual (a ritual we'll explore more fully later) that has developed around the grand opening of a Chick-fil-A restaurant. And their primary purpose for being there was to learn, from the president of the company, what Second Mile Service is, why it's so important, and what they can expect during their tenure with Chick-fil-A that will cause them to deliver Second Mile Service willingly and enthusiastically.

Chick-fil-A is a popular feature at shopping mall food courts, where it typically outsells in six days (they're closed on Sundays) its neighbors who are open every day. It's not uncommon to see a group eating together with three or four different food court brands represented at a single table. When a Chick-fil-A team member comes by a customer's table to clear away trash, and removes their friends' Sbarro plate and Wendy's bag, and then says, "My pleasure" when the surprised customers say, "Thank you," that's Second Mile Service. That takes Oomph!

OOMPH! SLAUGHTERS THE COMPETITION

In Randy Moss's case, opposing teams rue the plays in which Randy decides to show up. It seems that his quarterback merely has to get the ball airborne somewhere in Moss's ZIP code, and the guy is going to go up, catch it, and score, no matter how many opposing players are draped over his back. How he decides to celebrate after he gets in the end zone is another matter, but on those plays, he does get there.

Playing your "A" game is energizing and exhilarating. There is simply nothing like going flat out, throttle up, balls to the wall, playing with real passion and energy, especially in the company of others who are doing the same thing, and being part of a winning effort—a winning organization. Coming home after a day of playing your "A" game is like completing a hard physical workout in which you've given it all you've got . . . you're spent, but it feels great. You know you've done your best! No one can take it away from you.

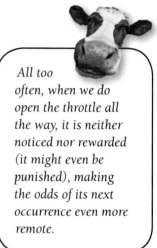

All too often, when we do open the throttle all the way, it is neither noticed nor rewarded (it might even be punished), making the odds of its next occurrence even more remote.

Everyone has an "A game." Each of us has things that we are passionate (or capable of being passionate) about. Some may not be terribly familiar with their "A" game because they haven't played at that level in a long time. Truth be known, most of us don't break out our "A" game very often. Instead, we spend much of our time operating on our "C" level—cruise control, if you will. All too often, when we do open the throttle all the way, it is neither noticed nor rewarded (it might even be punished), making the odds of its next occurrence even more remote.

OOMPH! LIGHTENS THE LOAD

The U.S. military is well-populated with people who routinely go above and beyond the call of duty. Command Sgt. Maj. Michele Jones—who was, until her retirement in 2006, the senior enlisted person in the United States Army Reserve—believes that's because there's a life-or-death connection between military personnel, as with police officers, firefighters, and a few other professions.

As she told us, "In a career field where a lackadaisical attitude can get either you or your battle buddy killed, the bottom line is this: Not giving your all can be deadly. That alone, for some people, increases their dedication, and perhaps redefines 'the call of duty.' We see it all the time on the battlefield. Soldiers going above and beyond, to lighten a buddy's load, to support the mission."[3]

OOMPH! GETS YOU MORE FOR YOUR MONEY

Rachel, a high school student, babysits for families to earn gas and spending money. She's good at her job, and, as a result, she's got all the work she can handle. One of Rachel's clients, Family A, is affluent, snobby, and treats her like the hired help that she, in fact, is. The relationship is strictly business. They're cordial, but there's no chit-chat, no "How are things at school?" kinds of discussions, and no apparent interest in Rachel as a person. They pay well (although they calculate the time to the quarter-hour), and lead an active social life, providing plenty of work for Rachel.

Family B is a little more down-to-earth. They treat her like one of the family. Although the hourly rate they pay is slightly less than that of Family A, they tend to round up, and have a generous interpretation of when Rachel actually arrived. In fact, lately, they've started paying Rachel a flat rate for the evening, regardless of when that evening begins and ends.

Rachel was sitting for the B's a couple of weeks before the senior prom, and as she left that night, Mrs. B pressed a couple of extra twenties into Rachel's hand and told her to go out and get herself something special for the occasion. One night, the B's stayed out much later than usual. When they arrived home, after 1 AM, a strong thunderstorm was in full fury. They offered to let Rachel spend the night at their house, but Rachel thanked them and opted to drive home. So Mr. B followed her just to make sure she got home OK.

Your babysitter and the kid who mows your lawn . . . in the same way that all working people do, *determine how much of their discretionary effort they are willing to invest.*

For many teenagers, their first employment experiences are of an entrepreneurial nature, representing their first foray into free agency. Your babysitter and the kid who mows your lawn determine their own standards of customer service, set their own wages, and, *in the same way that all working people do,* determine how much of their discretionary effort they are willing to invest in each job they're called on to do. This determination occurs somewhere in the background of our thought process on a task-by-task and moment-by-moment basis.

When Rachel gets a call from Family A, she checks her calendar, and her bank account as well. Right or wrong, that influences her decision to say yes or no. When she does say yes, she arrives on time (not early), and while she's there, devotes her attention 100 percent to the A children and their safety. She feeds them, changes them when needed, plays games, and puts them to bed. When the A's get home, they find the house in order, and the children asleep. They pay Rachel, and bid her good night.

Rachel's approach with Family B is somewhat different. She arrives early, to watch the kids while Mr. and Mrs. B get ready. She puts a little more into playing with the B children, and sometimes helps them with their schoolwork. After the kids have gone to bed, rather than just watching TV, she usually cleans up the kitchen, maybe runs a load or two of laundry, and does some tidying up around the house.

The B's get Oomph!; the A's get ugh.

OOMPH! TAKES THE "IM" OUT OF IMPOSSIBLE

In the spring of 2005, U.S. pharmaceuticals giant Pfizer undertook a significant reconfiguration of its sales force, partially in response to new legislation. This field force optimization, or FFO, required, among other things, a serious chunk of additional training for six thousand of the company's roughly ten thousand sales representatives. No mean feat. Many of us might have compared the magnitude of the task with the time and resources available, and declared the job impossible.

According to Stuart Rakley, senior director of Pfizer's Learning Strategies Group, the training had to be completed within a six-week window, with ten weeks of prep time, under "budget-neutral" conditions. You know what that means. Tim Kern, Pfizer's vice president of sales training, told us, "From the beginning, the prevailing attitude from everyone—management, support staff, and trainers alike—was, 'Somehow, we *will* do it. Let's figure out how.' Failure was never considered."

With Rakley as its leader, the FFO steering committee was responsible for preparing materials, creating customized learning plans for sixteen products, assigning faculty from among their in-house training staff (remember, no budget for outside trainers), and making sure that these six thousand people got to the right place on the right day, to receive the right training, having read the right materials beforehand. The employees had to be transported to Rye Brook, New York, comfortably accommodated, fed, and otherwise cared for, and returned safely home.

Everyone got in the game and played whatever role was needed, regardless of rank. There were lots of nights and weekends. A shuttle ferried people in from New Jersey at 5 AM, but there was no grumbling or whining. Everyone took it in stride. And for the most part, they enjoyed it. Bottom line: The effort was a complete success, budget-neutral and all.

You know the drill. We've all been faced with a task of seemingly insurmountable proportions. Some of those projects truly are insurmountable, but a lot of them somehow get done. Some don't. What makes the difference? In many cases, the critical success factor is the discretionary effort willingly contributed by a small (or sometimes large) group of people who care enough to make things happen, against all reasonable odds. Oomph!

CHAPTER SUMMARY

1. Discretionary effort, or Oomph!, represents the difference between what is required and what we're capable of doing. It's what is often referred to as "going the extra mile," "going above and beyond the call of duty," or "playing our 'A' game."
2. Though not backed by scientific research, our studies suggest that most of us have "C" game as our normal operating mode, and usually operate at less than 70 percent of our potential.
3. The decision whether or not to expend Oomph! in the workplace is a conscious matter, and it's personal.
4. Ugh represents the minimum level of human effort that is required, or perhaps tolerated, to give the appearance of getting the job done.
5. Oomph! is not overwork, or workaholism.
6. The benefits of Oomph! are:
   a. It's good for the customer.
   b. It's bad for the competition.
   c. It helps lighten the load for others.
   d. It gets you more for your money.
   e. It takes the "im" out of "impossible."

MONDAY MORNING, 8am

1. Take an honest assessment of your own tendency to expend discretionary effort at work. Rate yourself, on a scale of 1–10 (1=ugh, 10=Oomph!). Where can your effort meter usually be found? What would move the needle—up *or* down?

2. Recall a time when you were really motivated to give your all to some endeavor, job, cause, relationship, or whatever. What caused you to turn the throttle up?

3. Pick one leadership behavior that you know impacts the Oomph! of your team, and resolve to get better at it over the next, say, ninety days.

4. Make a commitment to finish what you've started (namely, this book), and learn what *you* can do to *give* more, and *get* more, Oomph! where you work.

2

WHENCE COMETH OOMPH!?

*Discretionary effort is like loose change in a person's pocket. It is
management's job to get them to want to spend it every day.*
—Russell Justice, technical associate and quality
consultant, ret., Eastman Chemical Company[1]

Why are some individuals able to operate in their "sweet spot" more regularly than others? How do some leaders tap into employees' reservoir of energy and enthusiasm while others seem ignorant of its very existence? What conditions trigger the expenditure of Oomph! and which ones turn the spigot off? How long can Oomph! be sustained? Can we replicate it, or is discretionary effort a mystical mojo that shows up when it shows up? Valid questions all, and we're going to do our best to address each of them, and more.

Our quest for answers to the above questions has led us to conclude that Oomph! springs from at least three sources:

1. **Our leaders.** Some leaders are able to coax more Oomph! from their followers than are others. How do they do it?
2. **Our organizations.** Some organizations—Pfizer, Chick-fil-A, and Marriott, for example—by virtue of their cultures, provide environments more conducive to the expenditure of Oomph! Others can't seem to get people to go even the first few yards without inducements they haven't earned, and that their employers can't afford. What makes the difference?

3. **Our nature.** Some people are just more likely to dispense discretionary effort, almost without regard to their leaders or environment. We call them "Extra Milers." We've met some of these people, and we're going to introduce them to you. We'll also help you recognize potential Extra Milers, so that you can attract them, hire them, and keep them engaged.

WHAT TURNS OOMPH! ON?

More often than your grocery bagger has asked the question, "Paper or plastic?" we have asked, in the course of writing this book, "What turns your Oomph! pump on? And what turns it off?" While our data in some cases may have been gathered using less-than-scientific means, the volume and consistency of it has led us to some clear, strong conclusions about just what it is that causes people to leave the Oomph! pumps on, or to switch them off.

"Oomph! ON" is the factory setting. Most people show up on day one ready to use it. We, as leaders, leave it on or turn it off.

Did you notice we said "leave on," not "turn on"? That is because, for most, we believe "Oomph! ON" is the factory setting. Most people show up on day one ready to use it. We, as leaders, leave it on or turn it off.

What causes people to give discretionary effort? Here's a compilation of the most consistently offered answers.

1. **I find the work itself interesting and pleasurable.** One of the most prevalent responses to our question centers on the nature of the work itself. People who find both the objective of the work and the tasks and duties involved intrinsically interesting and enjoyable are far more inclined to put themselves wholeheartedly into what they do.

Those who are fortunate enough to find work whose activities, at the very core, somehow stimulate the pleasure centers in their brains will overlook a host of unfavorable conditions in order to engage themselves in that work. For these workers, time passes at a faster rate. Most days, they actually look forward to going to work. Some would say they experience a "healthy high" (remember, we're not talking about workaholics here) that fuels their willingness to go above and beyond. This is different from working in a fun atmosphere. This is work that feels almost recreational. And work that feels like recreation is easier to throw yourself into than work that feels like, well . . . work.

My earliest experience with really interesting and enjoyable work was as an international telephone operator for AT&T Long Lines—what a cool job! This was in the late 1970s, when most overseas calls had to be placed through an international operator. Almost every call was an adventure. Some could easily take hours to connect, if they connected at all. This is hard to imagine in an age when we can flip open our clamshell cameraphones and dial practically any other phone on the planet.

Every day sailed by like the ocean liners whose ship-to-shore calls we often handled. Daily, I conversed with people all over the world, occasionally celebrities, one or two heads of state. You'd have thought Nicaraguan president Anastasio Somoza was a nice guy from talking to him. I understand he wasn't. No two days were alike. Call me crazy, but the job was just plain old, flat-out fun. We were busy. The work was challenging, and we all worked lots of overtime. Sure, I was tired on the twelfth straight day at the switchboard, but it was a "good tired." You know the feeling.

I gave this job my all. But it wasn't because I had a profound connection to the company's values. I was a twenty-year-old college student. I couldn't have cared less about AT&T's values, if it even had any. And my enthusiasm certainly didn't arise from being treated like an adult, with lots of discretionary decision-making authority. We had to place a flag—get this—a *yellow* flag above our position when we needed to pee!

Talk to any good computer programmer. Most will tell you they'd rather be at their terminal, cranking out cool code, than almost anywhere else in the world. Geeks? Maybe. Nerds? Sure. But happy? Without a doubt. The last few years have brought lots of news of commercial airline pilots taking pay cuts, going on strike, and threatening to strike. But if truth be told, most pilots would fly for free if they could afford it. They love flying that much.

Think about your own work. Do you absolutely love what you do? All of it? Most of it? If you're like most people, you throw yourself into those parts of your work that you really get excited about and, if you're totally honest, you'd have to admit that you keep a little effort in reserve for those tasks, and perform adequately at best on the others.

Wouldn't it be great if we could design a job that allowed us to spend most of our time doing the very thing we most enjoyed? Or if we hired people whose favorite work activity just happened to be the thing we needed them for most? Maybe we can.

DOWN 'N DIRTY

- To the degree you can, load jobs with core tasks that appeal to what the worker enjoys most.
- You've likely already grown accustomed to the notion of "mass customization" for your customers. Now consider it for your workers.
- Be careful not to "clutter" jobs with extraneous tasks that fit poorly with the worker's skills, talents, and aptitudes. Instead, assign those tasks to those who like doing them, or find a way to outsource them.

We're not suggesting that you take this to an extreme. Everyone has to do chores they don't particularly enjoy doing (just ask any restaurant server about their "side work.") But, take a close look at what your people spend time doing. How much of it really serves the core purpose of their jobs? Which tasks do they routinely avoid? Which tasks could be given to others who would thank you for the assignment? If your objective is to increase Oomph!, give this some thought, then act.

2. I was raised that way. Some people, by virtue of the values instilled and examples provided by their parents and others who've influenced who they've become, find it more natural to go all out, to do the best they can (not just what's expected) in almost everything they do. Call it guilt. Call it working to their values. Whatever it is, it works.

None of us as managers can reach back and control anyone's upbringing. But we can certainly be careful to populate our workforces with people who, insofar as we can determine, demonstrate a pattern of working with Oomph!

How can you tell if someone's likely to give Oomph! by virtue of who they are? One way is to look for evidence of volunteerism in applicants. Those who will work without pay, in pursuit of helping others, are more likely to be driven by the very motivators that stimulate Oomph!

We can certainly be careful to populate our workforces with people who, insofar as we can determine, demonstrate a pattern of working with Oomph!

When interviewing a job candidate, ask, "What is your passion? Tell me about a time when you were going flat out, hitting on all cylinders. What were you doing? What caused it? When was it? How long did it last? How do you feel about others around you who aren't going all out?" Pay particular attention to the answer to the question, "What caused it?" That will tell you a lot.

3. I don't want to let my team down. Peer pressure can be good for Oomph! No one wants to be the reason the project failed, the shipment didn't get out, or the department's production goal didn't get met. It's the old "rising tide raises all ships" thing. Teams with high standards naturally encourage some people to do more than they otherwise would, simply to avoid embarrassment. Rather than manipulation, or undue pressure, the dynamic of team expectations can often be the catalyst that ignites the spark of effort that lies dormant in some workers.

4. This is my calling. The word "vocation" comes from the Latin word "vocare"—to call. Certainly not everyone can work in their calling. It's probably safe to say that not everyone even *has* a calling. But those who do and whose life's work is in their calling report that they draw from an almost bottomless well of energy that they find deep inside themselves.

IN SEARCH OF YOUR SWEET SPOT

Doug Kimsal is a music minister in Gulf Breeze, Florida. While in his mid-thirties, he left a successful career as a vice president with a large information technology company, before it was fashionable to do so. He moved his wife and three children halfway across the country, attended seminary for two very lean years, and then began his ministry.

> *If you're called to do something, you'll put more into it than if you're just paid to do it* —Diane Raines, chief nursing officer, Baptist Health Systems, Jacksonville, Florida

He went from working long hours in the corporate world to even longer ones at the church. His home and lifestyle are more modest now than before. Yet he's never been happier with his work. "It's not a job," he said. "It's a calling. I found my sweet spot," he told us.

Says Kimsal, "I work way more now than I did when I was with the company. I think I'm up to, like, a buck-ninety an hour now, but you know what? You put in the hours, but it doesn't seem like you're putting in the hours."

Nancy Holland taught middle school for three or four years. "It takes a special kind of person to teach eleven- to fourteen-year-olds," she told us. "I'm not that special." At age thirty-four, still possessed of a strong desire to do something meaningful, but in a career that would eventually allow her lots of time at home with her children, she applied to nursing school. Three intensive years later, she found herself assigned to an ortho/neuro/trauma specialty floor at Erlanger Hospital in Chattanooga, Tennessee.

That was 1991. "I look forward to going to work for my three thirteen-hour shifts a week. I've never had the same day twice in these fifteen years," she told us. "The variety of the doctors, my co-workers, patients, and their families, plus the stimulating pace, make for days full of opportunity. Yes, the paperwork, threat of lawsuits, and patient expectations can be overwhelming, but with strong support from my supervisors, and lots of teamwork, I get invigorated instead. There are constant opportunities to learn and grow in this field. This is not the dreaded 'bedpan land' that some trudge into each day. For me, I've found more than a 'great job'—I'm living out my calling."

I recently ran into another dedicated person with a calling in a nursing home where my mom resided. While visiting and feeding her one afternoon, my dad and I chatted for a few minutes with Mary, a member of the nursing staff. When my dad asked Mary how she was doing, Mary, a cancer patient, replied that her doctor had recently given her six to twelve months to live, and encouraged her to quit her job and enjoy her remaining days. She became visibly upset, actually angry in recounting her physician's advice. "I'm not about to quit my job. These patients need me, and this place is my home," she replied. "This is what I do!" she added.

You don't have to work as a minister, nurse, or social worker to have a calling. Kathy Rockel has found her calling in helping professionals in the medical transcription field to be the best people they can be. No, she's not in human resources; she's a certified medical transcriptionist now serving as vice president of Transcription Relief Services (TRS) of Greensboro, North Carolina. TRS is "home" (the company motto is "Welcome Home") to about eighty-five very happy medical transcriptionists (MTs) in about forty U.S. states and a few countries in the Caribbean and South America.

Kathy left her previous employer frustrated and disillusioned with the medical transcription industry, a business that relies almost exclusively on a home-based workforce of people (primarily women) who transcribe physicians' dictated comments to become part of patients' medical records. More than 400,000 people earn their livings as MTs in the U.S., and the industry runs an employee turnover of about 50 percent annually. "People get very isolated," Kathy said. "Do your work . . . get your check. That's it."

Yet, consider the implications. The people in this job, which requires extensive training and certification, are responsible for quickly and *accurately* reducing to text the words that describe patients' histories, conditions, procedures, and other medical information. Getting it right is important. Often life-and-death important. It's not like the person in the drive-through getting your order wrong. This stuff matters, a lot. Yet, regrettably, the industry overall has failed to enjoy a reputation for being a great one to work in.

Ready to scrub her hands of the profession to which she had devoted most of her working life, Kathy told her friends, "I don't know what I'm going to do from here, but I'll never again work for a transcription service."

Famous last words.

"Then someone told me I should look into TRS—that they were different." (There's that reputation thing again.) "After a few visits at TRS, and meetings with company president Bob Harvey, I said, 'This is what I always thought a transcription service could be.' I always thought a company can be a good place to work, and still make money, and TRS showed me that I was right."

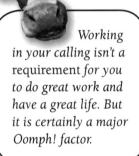

Working in your calling isn't a requirement for you to do great work and have a great life. But it is certainly a major Oomph! factor.

"Why is your job at TRS a 'calling'?" we asked.

"I'm able to do things at TRS that create real value for our MTs. I've been able to realize that dream that says, 'MTs are important; they're to be respected for their knowledge and skills. They can make a good living, have a good lifestyle, and not just be a number out there pounding out lines.'" (Medical transcriptionists commonly get paid by the line for their services.)

"And that makes all the difference in the world to me," she went on. "It's been great watching our leaders develop and mentor others. We have people who are doing things that no one would have imagined they could do. And that reaches my heart."

Michelle Smith is a vice president with O. C. Tanner, the U.S.'s largest employee recognition and incentives provider. Her calling is to help clients recognize great work in their employees, and she says that this calling provides a "fuel source" that motivates and sustains her. She's not in social work;

she's in business. But, says Smith, "the fact that my work is a calling elevates it to an entirely different plane."

The point is worth repeating—having a "calling" isn't reserved exclusively for those who toil in the fields of altruism. Some players in very profitable businesses help their companies earn lots of money precisely because the work they do—work that earns a profit—calls out to them. Finding your sweet spot, working in your calling, isn't a *requirement* for you to do great work and have a great life. But it is certainly a major Oomph! factor.

CHAPTER SUMMARY

1. Oomph! comes from our leaders, our organizations, and our nature.
2. Oomph! turns on when the work is interesting and pleasurable.
3. Oomph! turns on if you were raised that way.
4. Oomph! turns on when the team is depending on you.
5. Oomph! turns on when your work is your life's calling.

MONDAY MORNING 8AM

Refill your coffee (think Starbucks) and ponder the following questions:

1. Is your organization more a home for Oomphing, or ughing? How do you know?

2. How many of your people are working in their "sweet spot"? How can you increase this ratio?

3. How good a job are you doing of hiring people whose current operating mode is "Oomph! ON"?

CHAPTER

3

WHERE GOETH OOMPH!?

*Do you know how much faster I can fix an airplane when I want
to fix it than when I don't want to fix it?* —Gordon Bethune,
former aircraft mechanic and CEO, Continental Airlines[1]

WHAT TURNS OOMPH! OFF?

Oddly enough, this book is, in many respects, less about what inspires discretionary effort in our workers than it is about what turns it *off*. If you think that by this we're focusing on the negative, we'd argue that just the opposite is true.

As we pointed out before, most people start their career, and each job that comprises it, at an enthusiasm level that exudes Oomph! The default condition is ON. Ken Blanchard, in his now-classic work on Situational Leadership, points out that most people begin their jobs with relatively low competence but high commitment and enthusiasm. As the competence level increases and, we would argue, as managers and the organization get their hands all over the worker's psyche, that commitment level wanes, waffles, and, in some cases, craters. In Blanchard's model, it may take lots of time and the development of a great deal of competence before the worker achieves that groove where once again enthusiasm and commitment are high.[2]

So what is it that turns these pumps—whose natural state is on—off? The following are the most common responses we get.

1. My work doesn't seem to matter. When people begin to entertain the question, "What's the point?" their Oomph! pumps start shutting down. That happens when they doubt that their job has any real value to anyone—the manager, the team, the company, or most of all, their customers. This includes, but is not limited to, busywork. With alarming regularity, managers ask workers to direct their efforts toward one project or another, creating, for a while at least, the impression that the resultant work will be applied to solve a problem, realize some revenue, or serve a customer. The first time this scenario is played out, the worker may have exerted significant discretionary effort and proudly presented the finished product to the manager who requested it. When the product is then relegated to the shelf and never sees the light of day, the worker soon learns that it's not in his best interest to put too much into the next request.

> *When people begin to entertain the question, "What's the point?" their Oomph! pumps start shutting down.*

2. Priorities change too rapidly, and without evidence of good reason. I once had a boss who habitually sounded the trumpet to rally the troops to take a particular hill. We all dutifully marched toward the hill, poised to conquer the enemy. Then, while we were mounting the hill, he would sound the trumpet again and direct us not to take *that* hill, but the hill over *there*. We flailed from hill to hill, project to project, priority to priority, with dizzying velocity, expending tons of effort to produce little of significance. So predictable became his antics that before long, we learned not to invest much effort into any of his pet projects.

Leaders who inspire Oomph! are diligent to rout out every unnecessary movement, useless task, and fruitless endeavor that might work its way into a person's job.

3. My manager seems dispirited, pessimistic, or disengaged. Some people lose their Oomph! when their manager isn't around very much, or shows lack of confidence, optimism, or support. The world witnessed a perfect example of this when, for precious hours and days after Hurricane Katrina ravaged New Orleans, the city's mayor, Ray Nagin, was nowhere to be seen, holed up in his Hyatt Hotel room. We're given to wonder if the well-publicized meltdown of the city's police department would have happened had the mayor been more visibly engaged.

Probably more than any of us realize, workers watch the boss. They take their cues from their leaders, watching for signs of hope, despair, excitement, disappointment, confusion, and a myriad of other emotions that might affect the work environment, positively or otherwise. Managers are people, too, and can't be "up" all the time. When leaders have taken the time to build healthy working relationships with their people, their workers will forgive the occasional bad day. But chronic crankiness, lack of enthusiasm, or persistent pessimism will suck the Oomph! out of even the most committed and engaged of workers.

4. Quality, ethical, and performance standards are lax. In some companies, no one seems to care if the work is done particularly well, only that it gets done. This worker thinks, "If my manager doesn't care whether or not I knock myself out, I certainly don't."

Uneven expectations of quality are just as dispiriting. Hardworking people want to work in the company of equally competent, committed, and honest individuals. Workers will pull someone else's weight for a while, especially if there's a good reason, one that they understand. But they're loath to bear others' yokes for the duration of the journey. In the same way, when managers turn a blind eye to dishonest, unethical, or unprofessional behavior, there are complex

"If my manager doesn't care whether or not I knock myself out, I certainly don't."

and negative implications for discretionary effort. It sends signals you don't want to send. And it slows things down by diluting trust.

Don't fall into the "tight labor market" trap. One of the surest, fastest ways to tank Oomph! is by lowering your hiring and/or performance standards.

> *Everybody goes through three interviews. We don't just*
> *hire people off the street. We'll all work twice as hard for as*
> *long as we have to until we find the right one.*
> —Jeromy Williams, owner/operator, Chick-fil-A

5. I've lost the expectation of success. Not everyone can muster the hope of Thomas Edison, who reportedly tried thousands of filaments in his electric light bulb before finally landing on the one that lit up his life, and everyone else's. There is much to be said for perseverance, but at some point, everyone needs to believe that there's a light at the end of the proverbial tunnel.

One of the surest, fastest ways to tank Oomph! is by lowering your hiring and/or performance standards.

People need to experience success at reasonable intervals. This is one of the best arguments for hiring well, so that the people you put on the payroll have a fighting chance of being successful. In the same vein, if your existing workers have jobs that afford insufficient exposure to success, it may be time to redesign those jobs to up the chances of your employees getting at least a base hit, from time to time.

PRIDE COMETH BEFORE OOMPH!

If we've done most everything else right, we should have in place people who are eager to do good work, and proud of it when they do. Why is it then that so many of us manager-types hire seemingly competent, mature adults, train them as professionals, and then, over the course of their careers, treat them as though they had just graduated from daycare, deeming them incapable of rational, productive thought or behavior?

How do we do that? By:

1. Shoving a job description in someone's face whenever we want them to do something unpleasant, at which point they balk, predictably. And then we wonder why we hear the words "that's not my job" whenever we ask them to do something that's a little outside the job spec.

2. Having the audacity to run around telling our people they are "empowered" to do their work, and then placing ridiculous limits on their ability to fix problems and satisfy customers. When I checked into a hotel recently, I was greeted by a desk clerk wearing a button that said, "I'm Empowered." When I asked her what the button meant, she looked at it and said, "I don't know; they just told me to wear it." Come on! The woman isn't even empowered to accessorize her outfit, much less serve customers!

3. Having a "supervisor" for every six or seven worker bees. Are your people really that incompetent?

4. Bailing them out, or worse, taking over, when we see them struggling. "Oh, forget it. I'll just do it myself." We all need the benefit of some real-live-fire practice. As Mark Twain put it, "A man who carries a cat home by the tail learns ten times as much as one who only watches."

5. Insisting that we personally review/approve any information, recommendations, or reports that are destined for points north of us in the food chain.
6. Burdening well-intentioned people who usually demonstrate exceptionally good judgment with a "To-Don't List" of policies and procedures that causes them to lose any appetite they may have once had for using their brains.
7. Keeping on the payroll those who consistently demonstrate that they require the kind of supervisory oversight spelled out in items 1–6 above.

SUPERMAN SYNDROME

After nine years successfully operating an eight-color press in a large commercial printing plant, Tony was promoted to supervisor of the team of which he had been a member. Without any leadership training, or enunciation of expectations from his manager, he tackled the new job the best he knew how. Even though he was happy in his new position, he simply couldn't resist the temptation to rescue his team members from impending peril. Whenever a technical issue arose, or the colors appeared to be off-spec, Tony would figuratively don his Superman outfit, fly down to the plant floor, and save the day by personally fixing the problem.

Not surprisingly, his team members began to resent his behavior. A group assembled, went over Tony's head, and complained to the press manager that Tony was taking away their work. "He doesn't teach us how to do it; he just does it," was their summation of the situation. The manager (who clearly was remiss in not getting appropriate training for Tony before he assumed the new job) sat down and had an open, meaningful, and, we think, brilliant conversation with Tony.

"Tony, what part of your new job as a supervisor do you like the most?" asked the manager.

Without hesitation, Tony replied, "Production scheduling. Why do you ask?"

"How would you feel if I told you that I'd handle the production scheduling from now on? You can devote your time and attention to the other, less tedious parts of your job," said the manager.

"You gotta be kidding!" said Tony. "I'd hate it. I'd feel cheated . . . like my job wasn't important."

"Relax. I'm not going to take any of your work away from you. How do you think the guys on the floor feel when you run down there and fix the color problems, or the plates, or any of those kinds of things? I know they're not as good as you yet, but if you'll work with them, they'll get there."

The two gently bantered back and forth for a good half-hour or so, Tony bringing up short-term quality concerns, and the manager pressing his point about giving the operators back their work. Tony got it, instituted formal and informal training around color matching, and exercised a little more discipline about putting on that Superman outfit.

THE GREAT QUESTIONS OF OOMPH!

In the course of researching this book, we sought the answers to a limited and focused set of big questions, those questions being:

1. What is discretionary effort?
2. What are its benefits?
3. What stimulates it?
4. What stifles it?
5. What specific actions and behaviors can leaders engage in to get the most from it?

We've tried to answer the first four questions in the preceding pages. The answer to question five is woven into the entire fabric of what is to follow.

In an effort to ascertain what leader traits turn (or leave) the Oomph! pumps on—and what traits turn them off—we simply asked people, using a variety of methods. We polled a community of more than five thousand readers who subscribe to our monthly leadership newsletter, *Fresh Milk*. We asked executives, line and staff managers, human resources professionals, clinical and organizational psychologists, and, most significantly, workers—those people who make that determination every day as to how much, or how little, of their own discretionary effort they choose to employ. We interviewed seminar participants, people over the phone and via e-mail, and focus groups in various parts of North America. We put all of their input into a large cauldron, turned up the heat, stirred sufficiently, and here's what bubbled to the top.

OOMPH! BOOSTERS: LEADER TRAITS THAT TURN ON THE OOMPH!

1. Honesty and integrity
2. Competence
3. Taking real interest in teammates
4. Compassion
5. Authenticity
6. Optimism
7. Leading by example
8. Consistency
9. Communication (especially listening)
10. Fairness

So, if these things inspire Oomph!, just what is it that puts people in "C" game mode? What do managers do that causes workers to operate at less than their capacity? Our research and observations point to some very specific factors that get much of the credit for being performance blockers. Not surprisingly, some of them are antithetical to the above qualities.

OOMPH! BUSTERS: LEADER TRAITS AND TACTICS THAT TURN OFF THE OOMPH!

1. Not exhibiting or inspiring trust
2. Making employees believe they are being taken for granted
3. Poorly matching the person and the task (square pegs in round holes)
4. Offering misguided "rewards"

1. Not exhibiting or inspiring trust. Playing your "A" game involves risk . . . of failure, embarrassment, and at times, personal injury. Risk is inherent because you are trying to do things that you've never done before and, at times, things no one has done before. When you get down to it, we really don't know what our limits are, so "pushing the envelope" involves some risk and exploration.

On May 25, 2001, Erik Weihenmayer, with a team of nineteen other climbers and Sherpas, summited Mount Everest, setting a record for the largest group to successfully make the summit in a single day. As they had done before on Mount McKinley, Aconcagua, el Capitan, Kilimanjaro, the Ouray Ice Park, and other climbs, Erik and his team were playing their "A" game that day.

More impressive perhaps than the fact that such a large group had summited the mountain is the fact that, since age thirteen, Erik has been completely blind. That's right, blind. Lest you think otherwise, this was anything but an expedition where nineteen healthy climbers carried the blind guy up a mountain—Erik was as much an integral part of the team as anyone. With full faith and confidence that each member would do his part, dying if need be rather than let his friends down, this team was able to do what had never before been contemplated, let alone accomplished.*

Absent complete trust in our own abilities, and in the performance of those around us, it is impossible for us to play our "A" game. Instead, we reserve a certain amount of energy and effort, either as compensation or insurance against the perceived risks. We neither want to get screwed nor hurt, so we hold something back and, like a racecar driver on an unfamiliar course, we slow down.

Absent complete trust in our own abilities, and in the performance of those around us, it is impossible for us to play our "A" game.

Since 1988, we have asked survey respondents to agree or disagree with the statement: "I believe that most people here are doing their very best work." Over the course of more than 200,000 completed surveys in a diverse group of participating organizations, favorable response is right at 50 percent, suggesting that a lot of us are stopping our throttle levers well shy of "balls to the wall." With but a few notable exceptions, institutional trust (in the workplace) has been effectively gutted. Put a fork in it—it's done.

Somewhere around 1989, the landscape of the American workplace began a tectonic shift in which the last vestiges of the "paternalistic partner-ship" working arrangement crumbled—perhaps forever. Much of the cause and effect is described in Daniel Pink's excellent book, *Free Agent Nation*. The largely relational "Old Deal" construct, which was based on things like fealty to the organization, economic security, camaraderie, recognition, long-term advancement, and a sense of belonging, disappeared.[3]

In its place arose a "New Deal," a less relational and much more transac-tional construct in which the worker (at all levels) trades time and talent for the opportunity to score some cash, build a résumé, learn, and—with any luck—do meaningful work. Beyond the bounds of this construct, any sense of obligation to the organization pretty much vanished. Despite the normal

---

*Rather than resting on his laurels, Erik works regularly with blind youth around the world, helping them discover and achieve their own potential. We're proud of you, big E.

workplace class differences, this new arrangement is not confined to being a blue-collar or white-collar thing. It's the deal, period.

Though a short list of organizations regularly credited as being employers of choice has successfully bucked the trend, critical mass has long been reached. As renowned management scholar Charles Handy put it, "Organizations will still be critically important in the world, but as 'organizers,' not 'employers'!"[4] That is a profound statement, one that anyone in a leadership position would do well to read again, and think about for a few minutes. Organizers, not employers.

A Society for Human Resource Management and CareerJournal.com poll in 2004 revealed that only 28 percent of employee respondents and 23 percent of HR professional respondents rated the trustworthiness of the organization's leadership at the most positive end of the scale.[5] Though it runs a bit counter to the conclusions of the report authors, our sense is that, on the premise that you either trust someone or you don't, the poll suggests that people find about three-fourths of their organization's leaders only marginally trustworthy, at best.

Not unlike what happens in a marriage, taking someone (or their effort) for granted is an absolute deal breaker when it comes to the expenditure of Oomph!

Workers (we'll no longer call them employees) now make up their minds, on a much more personal basis, whether or not their leaders can be trusted, and if they are worthy of some expenditure of the worker's discretionary effort. In the majority of cases, the answer is no, in which case, they play their "C" game (cruise control).

2. Taking employees for granted. At one point or another, everyone has gotten the distinct impression that they (or their efforts) are being taken for granted. Often, it occurs in a personal relationship—witness the fact that 43 percent of first marriages end in divorce within fifteen years. At other times, it occurs at work.

It has happened to us, and no doubt to you. Now, close your eyes, take a deep breath, and go back to that feeling for just a moment. Try to recall what your inclination was at that exact moment in time. Was it to redouble your efforts, to give even more effort to the cause, or to power back a notch or two and say "screw it?" . . . That's what we thought. Not unlike what happens in a marriage, taking someone (or their effort) for granted is an absolute deal breaker when it comes to the expenditure of Oomph!

3. Round holes—square pegs. Playing your "A" game is, by definition, playing with passion, with zeal, with real purpose. To us, playing with passion is heavily dependent upon loving what you're doing, or, at the very least, loving why you're doing it. People simply don't expend discretionary effort for things they're not excited about, even when the duty is easy or comes naturally.

A member of my immediate family is in the United States Armed Forces, and in 2004–2005 served in the Iraq War as a member of the Army's Stryker Brigade. We can be assured that serving in the infantry, fighting insurgents and Saddam loyalists who place no value on human life, in a God-forsaken wasteland seven thousand miles away from home was not something he loved doing. Yet, this young man did his job with passion and energy, leaning forward nearly every step of the way, earning early promotions and being recognized by peers and superiors alike for meritorious service.

Why? Certainly not because of what he was doing, but *why* he was doing it. He's on a mission that involves raising his level of self-confidence, ultimately acquiring a marketable skill in a field he's interested in, and creating a good life for himself and his family.

In some (no, many) cases, we find ourselves faced with a basic incompatibility, either between humans, or between the human and the work. Face it, not everybody is cut out to be happy, productive, and successful for every job, and every job environment. Take the soldier in the aforementioned paragraph out of his uniform, shove him behind a desk for ten hours a day, and he'd be positively suicidal in a month, as would those around him.

This is not in any way, shape, or form a diatribe against diversity. But it is a fairly strong admonition that people whose interests, goals, and preferences are not aligned with their work and their workplace will almost never reach into their discretionary reserve, other than to escape the situation.

4. Offering misguided "rewards." Many years ago, I was meeting with my team for the purpose of discussing our recent employee opinion survey, and soliciting from the group ideas as to where we (and I in particular, as the group's leader) could do a better job. At one point, one of the team members asked, "Can I be frank?" "Of course," I responded, making a mental note to spend some quality one-on-one time with this guy to resolve whatever made him feel he even needed to ask.

He then made a point about my management style that has stuck with me to this day. To paraphrase, he said that morale within the team was generally good enough that any of them would be willing to give me anything I asked for, and take on any project assignment without quibbling or second guessing. "But," he continued, "my concern is this. We've got a good group here, a talented group with lots of energy and ideas. But it seems that every time we bring an idea to you, we come away with a new project to work on." He then noted that, to a person, they were kept pretty busy already, and that more projects weren't always what they were looking for. So, he continued, "If you want to see the flow of new ideas slow to a trickle, keep doling out assignments with each and every new idea." Wow, the guy was right! It *was* my modus operandi to effectively reward (punish) just about every new idea with more work.

OOMPH!—USE IT OR LOSE IT

Having spent hundreds of hours riding jumpseat on FedEx jets, I've been exposed (not always voluntarily) to what some have playfully termed "aviator logic." One piece of that logic suggests that there are several things that are absolutely of no use to a pilot, or anyone aboard the plane. Not necessarily in any order, they are:

1. The airspace above you
2. The runway behind you
3. Fuel remaining in the fuel truck
4. Airport approach plates that were left in your car, and
5. Airspeed you don't have

In the same vein, discretionary effort *not spent* is of no value. It can't be stored for use another day. You either expend it in the moment, or it is gone.

There is a pretty good pile of evidence to suggest that, at least in the traditional workplace, people are choosing (and it *is* a choice) to be less "engaged," to part with less and less of their Oomph! In a December 2004 Commerce Clearing House study, 305 human resource executives were polled on the incidence of employee absenteeism, indicating that, in recent years, the rate of unplanned absenteeism has increased from 1.9 to 2.4 percent.[6]

Either we accept the notion that the human species is getting sicker (it isn't) or something else is in play here. In that vein, the poll suggests that 62 percent of these unscheduled absences are for—surprise, surprise—things other than illness . . . things like family issues (23 percent), personal needs (18 percent), stress (11 percent), or an entitlement mentality (10 percent). Think about the last four times you took off, ostensibly due to illness. We're willing to bet that, on at least one of those occasions, illness was a secondary—if not nonexistent—factor.

In an essay entitled "The Amateur Revolution," Charles Leadbetter describes how many of us dutifully trudge off and ply our craft by day, returning home at night to engage with passion in our "dream work." Lead-

Discretionary effort not spent *is of no value. It can't be stored for use another day. You either expend it in the moment, or it is gone.*

better cites the growing legion of what he calls "Pro-Am technologists" who program commercial software for a living, but scare the hell out of Microsoft by "working on Linux in their spare time because the spirit of collaborative problem-solving appeals so powerfully." In other words, there is this pent-up urge to apply one's initiative and creativity that is seeking new outlets.[7]

Seb Potter, a Pro-Am open source programmer, puts it very effectively. "For me, work is the oddity. Work is a kind of compromise. I do work which is as close as possible to my passions to make working tolerable. But I feel most myself when I am doing this open source stuff. When I am doing this and give it my complete and full attention, then everything else around me fades away and dissolves and I become completely focused." Wow . . . talk about being in the zone.

CHAPTER SUMMARY

1. Oomph! Boosters: Leader Traits That Turn ON the Oomph!
   a. Honesty and integrity
   b. Competence
   c. Taking real interest in teammates
   d. Compassion
   e. Authenticity
   f. Optimism
   g. Leading by example
   h. Consistency
   i. Communication (especially listening)
   j. Fairness
2. Oomph! Busters: Leader Traits and Tactics That Turn OFF the Oomph!
   a. Not exhibiting or inspiring trust
   b. Making employees believe they are being taken for granted
   d. Poorly matching the person and the task (square pegs in round holes)
   e. Offering misguided "rewards"
3. Discretionary effort cannot be stored for later use. It is either expended in the moment, or it is gone.

MONDAY MORNING, 8AM

1. If the expenditure of Oomph! in your organization were improved by 10 percent, what would the impact be?

2. List three things you can begin doing today, on a sustained basis, to improve the application of Oomph! in your organization.

3. Which one of the aforementioned items are you going to begin working on *today*?

OOMPH! IN THE REAL WORLD

Nothing could be worse than the fear that one had given up too soon, and left one unexpended effort that might have saved the world. —Jane Addams

Oomph! abounds in all manner of places, likely and unlikely, where people make the choice to go the extra mile, for all the reasons enumerated in the preceding chapters. You see it often at a Disney resort, for example, when a cast member picks up a piece of trash that, in other places, might be left until the end of the day . . . or the end of time.

You don't see it, but it's there, when a computer programmer takes an extra five minutes to document, in detail, what's going on in a particular segment of program code, so that it will be readily apparent to the next programmer who comes along, months or years later, to maintain the program. Her extra five minutes saves hours of research and head-scratching, and has trickle-down operational implications for the program that stretch the mind's capacity to estimate.

Students at Langley High School in Virginia see it when they participate in the "Case Day" program within AP Government classes taught by Jim Catlette (Bill's brother) and Allison Cohen. On his own initiative fourteen years ago, Jim put together a program which each year, students follow a particular case that is about to be heard by the United States Supreme Court.

But they don't just follow it, they *live* it. After a considerable amount of study that often involves bringing the adversaries or other evidence into their classroom, the students participate in mock trials of the case with notable jurists like Ken Starr and Ted Olson who graciously volunteer their time, after an invitation by the teacher, Catlette, whom no one seems able to say no to. To top it off, students get to see the real case argued before the court, and meet with the justices.

The program requires hundreds of hours of unpaid time by the two teachers, who are pursuing their life's work with purpose and zeal.

While Oomph!, and regrettably ugh, can be found all over the place, we'd like to highlight in this chapter two organizations with which we've had some firsthand experience, and where you're likely to see a greater share of Oomph! than in many of their competitors. Spanning the geography of the United States, we've selected the northeast's Wegman's Supermarkets, and the California coast's Pebble Beach Company.

WEGMAN'S SUPERMARKETS

If you ever visit a Wegman's supermarket, you'll know in an instant that you're not in just any grocery store. You're in the presence of something special. Wegman's, the Rochester, New York–based supermarket chain, with 2005 revenues of more than $3.8 billion, has worked hard since its beginnings in 1916 to cultivate a loyal following, not only of customers, but also of workers.

A perennial presence on *Fortune's* esteemed list of "100 Best Companies to Work for in America," Wegman's ascended to the number one position in 2005. On the day the rankings were announced, eighty-six-year-old chairman Robert Wegman, son of the founder, said on a company videoconference that receiving this distinction was "the culmination of my life's work."

"The culmination of my life's work!" What this multimillionaire had been working for all his long life was not running a phenomenally successful business, amassing an untold personal and family fortune, or even seeing his name plastered on shopping centers all over the northeastern United States, but—get this—being recognized for being the best *employer* in the country!

Wegman died on April 20, 2006, at the age of eighty-seven, knowing he had presided over a truly *exceptional* organization, in almost every sense of the word. Not a bad way to spend a long, full life.

Superlative results. Operating a supermarket, doing it well, and doing it profitably is an exceptional achievement. On average, most supermarkets earn operating margins of around 3.5 percent. Wegman's makes about 7.5 percent.

Most supermarkets turn over 100 percent of their staff every year. One of every five Wegman's workers has at least ten years' tenure; nearly 3 percent have been there more than a quarter-century. Most supermarkets sell about $9 worth of stuff for every square foot of store space. Wegman's squeezes $14 from that same square foot, and their stores are double and triple the size of the average store!

> *The word that comes to mind when I think of Bob Wegman is heart. He put his heart into his business as well as into our community. This is a tremendous loss. Recently, I described Mr. Wegman as one of the new "George Eastmans" of Rochester. And that is exactly the company he keeps in Rochester's history.* —Robert Duffy, mayor, Rochester, New York[1]

But then most supermarkets don't send their cheese managers to Europe for ten days in search of the best vignotte their customers' money can buy. Indeed, most supermarkets don't even have a cheese manager. They just have cheese . . . and managers.

Working in a supermarket would hardly be anyone's dream job, you might think. Wages and benefits generally reflect the slim margins inherent in the industry. The hours are unattractive, the work is hard, many of the tasks less than scintillating. The cases of bottled water Wegman's stock people unload are just as heavy as those at Winn-Dixie. The cake pans have to be scrubbed just as hard at Wegman's as at Albertson's. And Safeway's unsold fish is no more fragrant than that at Wegman's. Still, Sara Goggins, a nineteen-year-old education student working part-time at the Wegman's in Penfield, New York, told a *Fortune* reporter, "I love this place. If teaching doesn't work out, I would so totally work at Wegman's."[2]

> *In addition to having more produce, dry goods, and cappuccino makers on the shelves, Wegman's has more Oomph! in the aisles.*

As will come as no surprise, given the premise of this book, we are persuaded that *the* overriding reason Wegman's has produced such superlative results is that it carefully cultivates the willing and enthusiastic participation of the vast majority of its 33,000 workers. In addition to having more produce, dry goods, and cappuccino makers on the shelves, Wegman's has more Oomph! in the aisles.

Lasting impressions. We had the great fun of visiting the Wegman's in Fayetteville, New York, a suburb of Syracuse, on one stereotypically cold winter day. Met by an entourage led by store manager Patrick Lynch, we were taken on the grand tour of the cavernous store during peak weekday grocery shopping time—between 4 and 6 on a Thursday afternoon. "That's when you can see us at our best," Lynch had said, in setting up the meeting.

We're veterans of "site tours," having been dutifully paraded through countless factories, restaurant kitchens, cubicle wards, plumbing supply warehouses, and the like, in the course of studying the industries we write and speak about. Usually, some perfectly polite and well-meaning associate, who knows how to get back to the front office without dropping breadcrumbs, is tasked with traipsing us around and pointing out the various sights and sounds along the way.

By contrast, Lynch, along with deli manager Stephanie Fehr, front-end manager Mike Terranova, HR manager Stephani Young, and assistant managers Enrico Fabrizi, Gary Mitchell, and Bill Murray, exuded button-bursting pride as they showcased what their people have created for their customers. Each member of the party was so excited to show us how they do things.

After we'd been shown a dazzling array of food, drink, and all manner of other products we'd never seen in a supermarket,

> *At Wegman's, and quite possibly at your place, much of the difference rests in demonstrating to everyone on the payroll that what he or she does is important. That it makes a difference . . .*

Enrico interrupted, "Of course, what we sell is great, but here's what I'm *really* proud of." He took us to the front of the store to show us a wall with a beautifully displayed assortment of written kudos from customers, each one referencing at least one specific store worker. When these notes come in (says Enrico, "We get them all the time."), he takes the time to prepare a handwritten thank-you note to the worker, and then displays the customer's note on the board. "My handwriting's lousy," says Enrico, "but no one seems to mind." No one gets these kinds of results—the financial ones, or the customer enthusiasm ones—without the benefit of better-than-average expenditure of discretionary effort from a willing workforce.

At Wegman's, and quite possibly at your place, much of the difference rests in demonstrating to everyone on the payroll that what he or she does is important. That it makes a difference, and that, even in some small way, their having come to work that day and *done their best work* has made life measurably better for someone. That's a hard case to make to someone who just "works in a grocery store." "But," says store manager Patrick Lynch, "when we hire people, we tell them, 'You will make a lasting impression on people through the work you do here at Wegman's.'"

A lasting impression.

Wegman's hires experts. The sous chef at the Pittsford store, the chain's highest grossing at more than $2 million in sales per week, was recruited from The French Laundry, the famed Napa Valley restaurant.

And Wegman's creates experts. Assistant manager Bill Murray says, "Educated employees are the key to it all. There's a lot more to this [working in a supermarket] than most people would think. We have to train, train, train, and constantly be educating our people every day. Nobody wants to answer a customer's question with 'I don't know.'"

Wegman's goes to extraordinary lengths to train their people, to reap the extraordinary benefits that filter down to its bottom line. The company's philosophy holds that it's not about buying groceries. It's about enjoying the experience that comes with what you buy. What good is it to the customer to buy a beautiful piece of beef if the ultimate experience—the meal—wasn't so great? Says Murray, "We like people to come back and buy stuff again. Anything wrong with that?"

One is tempted to assume the cynic's position and rationalize that the family was just putting on its best performance for the invited guests (self-invited, we hasten to add). Had we been posing as ordinary customers, our experience would certainly have been different.

Extra Miler: Ben—We thought of that. And so, before our appointment, I simply walked into the store, like the hundreds of others that day, and pretended to do a little shopping. I subjected an unsuspecting stock person, a young man named Ben, who appeared to be a high school student working part-time in the store, to what I consider to be the ultimate test. I asked him where I could find a can of french-fried onion rings. You know, the kind whose only apparent purpose in life is to rest atop green bean casseroles. This is, quite possibly, the most obscure and difficult grocery item to locate in any supermarket. It doesn't really fit with anything else. It doesn't really belong with the canned vegetables; it's hard to place with potato chips or other salty snacks. It could be on an endcap, but in a huge store like this, finding it could take hours.

The young man behaved as though he had been waiting for the question. We can only imagine how many different items are kept in the 123,000 square feet of this store, and yet Ben had it cataloged in his brain to the aisle and shelf. Now, I don't know about you, but when I ask a supermarket stock person where I can find an item, I assume that they'll tell me just that—where *I* can find it, not where *they* can find it. In the best of cases, the person will rattle off an aisle number, perhaps, point in a general direction, and then wish me Godspeed.

Ben, instead, said, "Sure. Come with me." We mused at how canned fried onion rings are the hardest thing to find in the store. He agreed, and added that the only time he had ever eaten them was on top of green bean casseroles that his mom makes with, as I gathered, more frequency than he would like. More than a dozen aisles away, Ben homed in on the canned rings, asked me how many I wanted (I said one), and placed the can in my hand. Cha-ching. Forty-nine cents! Three cents to the bottom line.

Turning on the Oomph! After our invigorating tour of the store (after which, we must admit, we were starving), we sat down with the management team to find out what, in their view, allowed Wegman's to be on the receiving end of such copious measures of discretionary effort from so many of their people.

Here are some notes from the meeting:

- **The leadership, at the top.** Meaning the Wegman family. As big as the company has grown, the owners have remained true to their values. And because the company is family-owned, and doesn't have Wall Street breathing down its neck, Wegman's treats its workers the way they want to. And it has paid off. Bob Wegman said (and he actually *believed* it), "We can't serve the customer well until we've served our employees."
- **High standards.** There is tremendous pride in the Wegman's brand. The company vigorously protects and maintains those high standards in everything they sell, and everyone they employ.
- **Flexibility.** We were more than a little astonished to learn that this one grocery store has more than 750 people on its payroll! And yet, they find time to treat each one of those 750 people as an individual. They do a lot to keep people, and to keep them happy. And it pays.

  As an example, the Fayetteville store had a man on staff who happened to be from the Philippines. He liked working there so much that he recruited a number of family members to work in the store, and other Wegman's stores in towns where he had family.

One of his sisters, still living in the Philippines, and whom he hadn't seen in years, came to visit family in Maryland, and he badly wanted to spend some time with her. Rather than requiring him to take vacation, they simply plugged him into the store in Maryland, where he was needed to do the very same job he did in his home store. He worked all day and spent time with his sister in the evenings and on weekends. He didn't have to take vacation, he didn't lose any income, and it worked out great for Wegman's.

- **Personal attention from every department head.** Each department is like a family, with the department head as the head of the family. He or she makes the effort to get to know each member of the family, and learns how to get maximum effort from each one.
- **Managers are held accountable.** Managers are accountable for how well they treat their people, and how well they develop them. Senior management looks at the performance evaluations of each person, and asks about each department head, "How are their people doing on their evaluations, over time? Do their people get promoted? Do they go from part-time to full-time?"

Wegman's has made a lasting impression on millions of shoppers, and on us. It remains one of the best examples we've seen of extraordinary performance through ordinary people going the extra mile. Here's another.

PEBBLE BEACH COMPANY

The word "lagniappe" is a Creole-inspired term meaning a little something extra. It is often used in the hospitality industry when the guest is given a little more than they expect—an extra beignet when purchasing a dozen, for example, or a complimentary dessert or glass of wine with dinner. For our purposes, we feel the term is equally applicable outside of strictly commercial transactions. One sees it in the level of service provided by employees who are focused, fired up, and capably led. They seem more inclined to display a little extra effort. That is especially the case at Pebble Beach, a place that reeks of professionalism, and in turn, higher effort—*lagniappe*.

Upon passing through the gates to Pebble Beach, you know instantly that you are in a special place. The crisp sea air, rugged coastline, cypress trees, and birds—not to mention the heightened anticipation of playing a round of golf on the same ground where all the big shoes from the world of golf have walked—all assault one's senses.

But that's just the warm-up. Whether it be the shuttle drivers who ferry guests between nearby Monterey Airport and the Pebble Beach Company resorts, the front door staff at the Inn at Spanish Bay, massage therapists at the 22,000-square-foot spa, the incredibly nice phone operators who provide wake-up calls to guests, or the gardener at the luxurious Casa Palmero, one simply cannot miss the signs that the 1,800 or so workers who call this place home for eight hours per day have also bought in to the fact that it is special. The uniforms are crisp, the manners ever-present and sprinkled with a dose of California coastal charm, the smiles genuine, and the efforts to please constant.

> *Money can buy you a fine dog, but only love will*
> *make him wag his tail.*   —Kinky Friedman

We've been fortunate to visit the resort on a fairly regular basis over the last few years, as a supplier of management consulting services to the Pebble Beach Company. During that time, we've stayed on our dime as well as theirs. We've seen them in action as both regular guests, and behind the scenes. It doesn't matter. The experience simply does not change. So, other than a killer location, what do they have going for them?

Politeness. These folks are unfailingly polite, period. Whether they are serving you one of those delicious $18 Tap Room burgers, or perhaps disagreeing with you in a management presentation, the men and women of the Pebble Beach Company are exceptionally well-mannered. It's not an act, but a habit—something that was baked in long before they showed up for work at the Pebble Beach Company. It is clearly a quality that Susan Merfeld and her HR staff are serious about finding in each and every new recruit. When asked how they screened applicants for this quality, Susan replied, "We're looking for it early and often in the process."

Attitude. Though far from having a "chip on the shoulder," employees seem to have that extra assuredness that comes from knowing that they are playing on a championship team—that little extra bounce in the step that comes from the realization that others (lots of others) would love to be working in this same place, and on the same team. A shuttle driver who asked not to be named remarked that there were probably thousands of people living on the Monterey Peninsula who would like to have his job driving guests back and forth between the airport and the resort in a spanking new Lexus. "Truth be known, this is such a great job, if I could just have the benefits, I would do it for free," he said.

The little stuff. At Pebble Beach, they sweat the details—all of them. I learned this about an hour before our very first presentation to the company's management team, when I was asked to make a slight change to my Power-Point presentation, which CEO Bill Perocchi had just reviewed. It seems that the legend title on one of the graphs on one of the slides was slightly (make that minutely) askew, and Perocchi wanted the thing made right before his management team viewed it. That was the first of many lessons I've received on how far these folks go to make sure things are done right.

Pebble Beach management realizes that while life is beautiful on the Monterey Peninsula, it can also be hard, unless one is financially well-endowed. While they cannot reduce the cost of living or confer millionaire status for their employees, one thing they do with a vengeance is listen to employees, then make serious commitments to employee benefits and other programs that have the effect of removing many of the things that people worry about. Things like healthcare (medical, dental, and vision care are free) and free meals served daily to all staff in one of the employee dining rooms. Employees and their families are also able to visit the Health and Wellness Center, and receive free, top-notch medical care from a family practice physician and a staff of healthcare professionals.

"They run a lean ship, but they have the courage and foresight to invest, and are absolutely committed to making sure people have what they need to do their very best work."

Extra Miler: Dr. Eugene Benjamin—Eugene Benjamin, MD (Dr. B. to the Pebble Beach staff), who runs the Health and Wellness Center, has used the company's "let's get it done" mindset to take the delivery of healthcare to a whole new level. According to Dr. Benjamin, "Bill Perocchi (CEO), Cody Plott (president), and Dave Heuck (CFO) are businessmen first, and they run a lean ship, but they have the courage and foresight to invest, and are absolutely committed to making sure people have what they need to do their very best work." According to Benjamin, this results in him "being able to practice the best possible care that I'm capable of."

And practice it he does, in a way that most of us have never seen. Upon entering Dr. Benjamin's cramped office in the back of the Wellness Center, one can't help but notice two things:

1. His features, notably his smile, completely bald head, and big brown eyes, and
2. An entire wall covered with photographs of the center's patients, specifically the children of employees.

Off-the-record queries of Pebble Beach employees (who have the option to be treated where they want) revealed glowing praise for Dr. Benjamin and his merry band. "My wife wouldn't see anybody but Dr. B.," one staffer intoned. Another was quick to point out that as far as he was concerned, the main thing with Dr. B. was that "he cares," a remark that is borne out by the fact that the good doctor regularly makes it a point to reach out to patients by phone after a visit to see if the prescribed treatment or medicine is working, and the patient is feeling better. Another person described a situation when Dr. Benjamin made a weekend house call to treat her sick daughter. (Never mind the house call, *when was the last time your physician called to see how you were doing?*)

Dr. Benjamin allowed that "when you are surrounded by people who care as much as these folks do, you can't *not* take it to the next level."

Sense of purpose. Nowhere (repeat, nowhere) have we seen a workforce that is as focused like a laser on what they are about as the people at Pebble Beach. Employees not only can recite the company's mission statement, they are also comfortable articulating its essence in their own words. More important, their efforts to bring it to life are constant.

Extra Miler: Hubert Allen—Within five minutes of meeting up with Hubert Allen and joining him in his "office" aboard a golf cart on the Pebble Beach golf course, I felt that I had gotten a pretty good read on him. Golf shop manager of the famed Pebble Beach Golf Links, Hubert is known as one of the company's "go-to" guys. With a smile and a kind word to everyone, he seems to glide through a never-ending stream of issues with the coolness that one might expect from a seasoned Army veteran. As one of his peers put it, "If there is anybody around here we ought to clone, it's Hubert."

Despite the magnificent surroundings, his job is doubtless one of the tougher ones around. As golf shop manager, one of his main responsibilities is to ensure that every ten minutes a foursome of golfers departs the first tee of the course, that over the next four and a half hours they have the golfing experience of a lifetime, and that they maintain a pace of play that permits the players behind them to enjoy their rounds as well.

With each player wanting to soak in the surroundings and hit every shot perfectly, the "pace of play" thing becomes an issue that Hubert and his team of course marshals and caddies contend with constantly. "It's not easy telling four guys who have each paid $450 to play this course that they need to speed up so the players behind them aren't kept waiting," he said. Yet he does it, and does it well—really well. "Nice shots, gentlemen," he said to the four slightly off-schedule players departing the 13th tee. "You keep hitting them like that, and you're really going to enjoy your round, and so will the folks behind you."

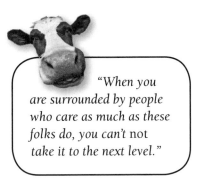

"When you are surrounded by people who care as much as these folks do, you can't not take it to the next level."

To Hubert, it's personal. "Whether it's a team member, a guest, or a vendor, I feel I need to connect with them on a personal level before I have any credibility to ask them to do something." Continuing, he added, "You know, some of your best lessons in life are learned from failure. I felt that I was a good soldier, a good sergeant, but my guys weren't sad to see me leave. I learned from that experience."

As we rode around the course, Hubert made it a point to warmly greet every guest and employee we encountered. It wasn't for my benefit. It's clear that this is his well-practiced habit. Though the pats on the back and chatter from Hubert flow freely, they are anything but idle. Rather, they are thoughtful, and there's a purpose there. The "how's it going?" to one employee is meant to gauge how the guy is doing in recovering from the recent death of his wife. The "what's up, Rocket?" is intended to acknowledge that he is aware that the caddie (they all seem to have nicknames) is having a tough morning. Even the comment to the tardy foursome was held until after they hit their tee shots so he would have a better chance of incorporating a compliment into the encouragement to pick up the pace.

CHAPTER SUMMARY

1. Two places to spot Oomph! in action are Wegman's Supermarkets and the Pebble Beach Company.
2. It's easy to see why Wegman's has been near or at the top of *Fortune's* Best Places to Work list for several years:
   a. All levels of leadership make employees a top priority.
   b. There is tremendous pride in the Wegman's brand.
   c. The hallmarks of their people practices are flexibility, personal attention, and employee recognition.
3. Pebble Beach Company has also cultivated a brand as an employer, not just a destination golf resort. What makes Pebble Beach special:
   a. They hire politeness and a "championship attitude."
   b. They sweat the small stuff, for their guests and employees alike.
   c. Their people have a sense of purpose that fuels their discretionary effort.

MONDAY MORNING, 8AM

1. Visit a place that's known as an employer of choice, like Wegman's or Pebble Beach. Observe from the employee's point of view. What do you see that distinguishes it as a *workplace?* What elements could you replicate?

2. Do you *have* a strategy designed to encourage more discretionary effort from people? Or are you just wishin' and hopin' for it?

3. Make it a point to get to know everyone on your team well enough to know what turns each of them on, and off. Like Hubert Allen, do something to connect with everyone you work with, on a personal level, to earn credibility.

SECTION TWO

BEFORE OOMPH!

CHAPTER

5

A LEADER TAKES TIME

*Things which matter most in life should never be at the mercy of
things which matter least.* —Johann Wolfgang von Goethe

You can't expect others to follow you, let alone part with their discretionary
effort, until and unless you've gotten your own act squared away. How well
you manage your time and priorities is an essential element in this process.

For the most part, leadership is a fairly simple proposition—not easy by
any means, but not complex, either. That means it is well within the grasp
of most of us who are willing to put the time in to do the essential tasks of
leadership. We use the expression "put the time in" advisedly, and in this
case it seems absolutely appropriate. Leadership is about taking the time to
do a bunch of stuff that, in the moment, may not seem especially fun or all
that consequential, but whose cumulative effect over time—especially when
observed by others (those being led)—ends up making a big difference in
how enthusiastically people perform.

What kind of stuff, you ask?

- Taking a few minutes of quiet time to establish a game plan for each day.
- Taking time to look out for your own health and well-being.
- Taking time to do something to actively recruit new people each day.
- Taking time to prepare and deliver thoughtful, honest performance reviews.
- Taking time to call someone you haven't seen in a while and ask how they
  are doing.

- Taking time to send someone a congratulatory note or thank-you card.
- Taking time to "go sit on a footlocker"[1] (this idea is described in chapter 11).
- Taking time to show up, in person, when someone on your team is facing difficulty.
- Taking time to go to training with your people instead of just sending them.
- Taking time to go watch your people work, and show them how they can do better.
- Taking time to make sure the communication pipelines are open.
- Taking time to help out a peer who needs it, but won't ask.
- Taking time to coach or mentor those who need or deserve it.
- Taking time to have some fun.
- Taking time to let someone know he or she is doing a good job, or screwing up, as the case may be.
- Taking time to talk with people about things that are important to them.
- Taking time to find out what your people's goals and aspirations are, and what makes them tick.
- Taking time to show up personally to deliver bad news.

After the events of September 11, 2001, despite all the other things he had to do, New York mayor Rudy Giuliani took time to do some things that were unpleasant and that could easily have been overlooked or delegated to others. Specifically, he made it a point to attend the funerals of scores of city employees (chiefly firefighters) and others who were killed in the attack. When asked about this in an Academy of Achievement interview, Giuliani said:

> It helped me to attend all those funerals and memorial services. I felt—and still feel—a tremendous amount of grief and pain about what happened. I lost very, very good friends. I lost people I had promoted, appointed, worked with, been through really horrible situations with, and I felt a great deal of grief. And to be able to share that with people and to help them in some way. . . . As the mayor of New York City, I used to go to police and fire funerals, and I knew from early on that being there helped people a lot. Not because of me personally, but because of my office, because it said something about the importance of the person and what they did.[2]

Sadly, a lot of the time-consuming stuff in our lives doesn't get done. Oh, it's not because we view it as unnecessary or fail to see the benefit. It doesn't get done—or done well—because we don't take the time to do it. We tell ourselves and others that the reason is that we "didn't have the time." In point of fact, we have all the time there is . . . 1,440 minutes per day, every day . . . the same amount of time that Gandhi, Martin Luther King Jr., Ronald Reagan, Mother Teresa, John Kennedy, Ben Franklin, and Marie Curie had. There isn't going to be any more of it. What we choose to do with that time is a function of our choices (mostly) and, in a few cases, circumstances legitimately beyond our control.

In point of fact, we have all the time there is . . . 1,440 minutes per day, every day.

Time-management gurus have for years maintained that, in reality, one cannot manage time at all. Rather, the best we can hope to do is manage those events that consume our time. But how?

IF NOT ME, WHO?

First, we must be clear-eyed in determining which events we really need to be directly engaged in, and which can be handled by others. It helps to have an internal bias toward using delegation to stretch and grow others. Bear in mind, though, that delegation involves not just asking someone to do something, but monitoring progress and ensuring that the task actually gets done. Not unlike the auto repair business in which an incomplete or insufficient repair causes the vehicle to come back to the shop (a "come back"), wise leaders also take pains to avoid "come backs" on delegated work.

Responsible delegation involves more than just passing out assignments of things to do—a lot more. It involves clarifying what is to be done, by whom, when, and what tools and resources might be needed to accomplish the task. It involves making sure people have the authority to accomplish the task and that they understand and accept the accountability that goes along with it. We highly recommend reading William Oncken's classic article "Management Time—Who's Got the Monkey?" first published in 1974 and reprinted in the November 1, 1999, issue of *Harvard Business Review.*

DOWN 'N DIRTY

Giving Up Control: Delegation (8 Levels)

Level 1: Get the facts; I'll decide.

Level 2: Suggest alternatives; I'll decide.

Level 3: Recommend an alternative; I'll decide.

Level 4: Decide; wait for my approval.

Level 5: Decide; act unless I say no.

Level 6: Act; report results.

Level 7: Act; report if unsuccessful.

Level 8: Act; reporting not needed.

JUST SAY NO

Much of our problem with time, er, event management ties directly back to over-commitment on our part. Not unlike politicians who just can't say no, we guarantee under-delivery by over-promising. Our sense is that most people are a lot more understanding of someone who promptly and politely declines a request for his or her time than of someone who agrees to do something, then bails out on the commitment, often at the last minute.

Just as the U.S. Forest Service has determined that some fires are best left alone, there are fires that we should let burn themselves out. Not every voice mail or e-mail needs a response. Not every crisis is truly urgent or deserves our attention.

There are fires that we should let burn themselves out. . . . Not every crisis is truly urgent or deserves our attention.

Wise managers are finding that one of the best things they can do to develop their staff, not to mention preserving their own sanity, is to occasionally let the staff know that they are going to be "untethering" (turning off phones, pagers, and e-mail) while they are away from the office. It's amazing how much stuff people can get done by their own devices when they realize that seeking permission or getting a lifeline is not an option.

PRIORITIES, PRIORITIES

At the end of the day, making the best use of one's time probably hinges more on having a clear sense of priorities than anything else. Without that bedrock, we quickly, inevitably find our time eroded by what Charles Hummel referred to as the "Tyranny of the Urgent." In his essay by the same name, Hummel used the typical human reaction to the ringing of a telephone as an example of how we will quickly abandon more vital endeavors in order to deal with the "urgent" need to put a stop to that incessant, irritating ringing noise.[3] Imagine what Hummel would have had to say in a world replete with e-mail, cellphones, pagers, and the like.

"Your greatest danger is letting the urgent things crowd out the important."

According to Hummel, the issue is not so much a shortage of time as a problem of priorities. Or, as a cotton mill manager once told him, "Your greatest danger is letting the urgent things crowd out the important."

We don't care whether you use the A-B-C prioritization method espoused by the FranklinCovey folks, or someone else's 1-2-3 method. The bottom line is that it is imperative that you operate with a clear sense of your long-term goals, together with a current set of near-term priorities that are balanced in favor of the big picture. On a daily (if not more frequent) basis, you need to sort out your intended activities according to their relative importance in the scheme of things. Our own personal prioritization categories include the following:

A. Mission critical
B. Important
C. Nice to do

Setting the priorities is the easy part—easy, but necessary. Then, you have to pay attention to what you have designated as most important. Your list is kinda like the lane markers painted on a highway. You should glance at it every once in a while to make sure you're tracking as planned—that the "A" stuff is getting done before anything else. And yes, before you ask, you really oughta write this stuff down, be it on a gum wrapper, in a planning journal, or on a PDA. If for no other reason, it gives you a feeling of accomplishment at the end of the day to sit down and cross off the day's achievements.

Whether done with a pencil or a cursor, crossing those items off is such a powerful experience that most folks who have accomplished something that was not originally on their list will actually write it down, for the sole purpose of getting to draw a line through it. You know who you are, and we've been watching ☺!

> *He that is everywhere is nowhere.*   —Thomas Fuller,
> seventeenth-century historian, scholar, and author

CHAPTER SUMMARY

1. Leadership is about taking the time to do things that make a big difference in how enthusiastically people perform.
2. You have all the time there is. There isn't going to be any more of it.
3. There is no such thing as time management. The best you can do is to manage those events that consume time.
4. Event management can be aided considerably by:
    a. Effective delegation to others (tasks, responsibility, authority, and accountability).
    b. Letting some fires burn themselves out.
    c. Diligently setting and adhering to goals-based priorities.

MONDAY MORNING, 8AM

1. Order a copy of William Oncken's classic article, "Management Time—Who's Got the Monkey?" (available from *Harvard Business Online*).

2. Revisit your list of prioritized daily tasks (you *do* have one, right?) and work nonstop on one of the "A" priorities for an hour. Do it now.

3. Select one of the "Taking Time To . . ." items and resolve to do it today.

Maybe turning one day into the next passively is all you have to do to mess up your life. —Liz Murray, professional speaker[4]

CHAPTER

6

TRUE NORTH

*To develop that special trust, a commander must win the loyalty
of his subordinates. Their loyalty will follow very naturally
if the commander offers his undivided loyalty to them in the
first place.* —Col. Ian R. Cartwright, U.S. Air Force[1]

People don't ordinarily commit chunks of their discretionary effort without cause, or on behalf of those they find lacking in some important respect. More to the point, they won't follow them period, let alone part with their Oomph! That is especially the case when it comes to those who lack—or have lost touch with—the essential, character-related qualities of leadership.

One of those qualities—indeed the very foundation on which this thing called leadership rests—is the expectation that a leader has a relatively accurate moral compass and can be trusted by those who would follow him or her to reliably do the right thing, even in the absence of guidelines. Make that *especially* in the absence of guidelines.

We're not talking about do-gooders, but about ordinary people who—when under the pressure of danger, threats, or temptation—manage to maintain an abiding sense of right and wrong. They are comfortable in their own skin.

RIGHT IS RIGHT

One of the reasons most of us have so little faith in our political "leaders" is that many of them seem perfectly capable of rationalizing any position on just about any subject in order to inflate their reputations, advance their agendas, or save their hides. Often, this is done through the careful parsing of words. One of Bill Clinton's all-time classics:

> "It depends on what the meaning of the word 'is' is. If the—if he—if 'is' means is and never has been, that is not—that is one thing. If it means there is none, that was a completely true statement."[2]

While decision making can be difficult—owing to the need to take into account a realm of facts and opinions—it is still quite possible, and indeed necessary, for leaders to maintain integrity at a high level. Adm. James Loy, U.S. Coast Guard, ret., addressed the matter in his essay entitled "The Moral Dimension":

> Our "honor" value . . . implies integrity at the 100 percent level . . . no blurring of the clear line between right and wrong. I believe that an otherwise high-performing sailor of any rate or rank that suggests there is no right or wrong because "it's all relative" poses a threat to sound ethical judgments. He or she, taken to the extreme, can "understand" 2nd Lt. William Calley Jr. at My Lai or even the actions of Adolph Eichmann.

> We must be constantly vigilant to identify right from wrong clearly and try never to let right get lost in the shuffle of commander loyalty or image-building or even our constant drive for success. RIGHT is RIGHT. It is our ethical TRUE NORTH. It goes to our personal and organizational values, values that we must protect and nurture for they are constants in an otherwise confusing array of choices.

> As he was sentenced for his Watergate role, Jeb Stuart Magruder lamented, "Somewhere between my ambition and my ideals, I lost my ethical compass. I found myself on a path that had not been intended for me by my parents or my principles or my ethical instincts." The cold realization of that truth must be devastating to the person who has strayed.[3]

AN ACCUMULATION OF LITTLE ONE-OFF DECISIONS

For years, Canadian-born Bernie Ebbers was viewed as a wonderboy as he grew a tiny Mississippi phone company into a telecommunications power-house through a series of highly leveraged acquisitions. Legend has it that Ebbers and his business partners had sketched out the plan for their long-distance phone company (LDDS) on a napkin in a Hattiesburg, Mississippi, coffee shop.

With commercials featuring basketball *überstar* Michael Jordan and the $40 billion acquisition of MCI in 1998, WorldCom was the darling of Wall Street. Things seemed great until June 25, 2002, when Ebbers's MCI WorldCom announced that, due to what later proved to be fraudulent accounting irregularities of gargantuan proportions, the company would need to restate earnings. When the dust finally settled, the restatement amounted to $11 billion, and MCI WorldCom's subsequent bankruptcy filing wiped out thousands of jobs and billions in shareholder wealth. In July 2005, Ebbers was forced to surrender much of his personal wealth and was sentenced by a federal judge to spend effectively the rest of his life in prison.

> *"Firms like Schwab don't get into trouble because somebody at the top decided one day that conflicts of interest are OK . . . but because of an accumulation of little one-off decisions."*

What happened? What went wrong? Though it is difficult to ever really know what is in a person's heart, there is a pretty good trail of behavior to suggest that Bernie Ebbers didn't wake up one morning and decide to pull off one of the greatest train robberies in history. No, it seems far more probable that Ebbers—the former basketball coach, Sunday school teacher, and gentleman farmer—had succumbed to the cumulative influence of what former Schwab CEO David Pottruck called a bunch of "little one-off decisions."

Speaking of difficulties his own firm had encountered during his tenure as CEO, Pottruck allowed that, "Firms like Schwab don't get into trouble because somebody at the top decided one day that conflicts of interest are OK . . . but because of an accumulation of little one-off decisions."

Whether the cheating started as a result of a little white lie to investment bankers, a little something extra on an expense report, or the tendency to start believing one's own marketing hype, chances are the great WorldCom meltdown started low and slow and worked its way up from there. The lesson for the rest of us who would accept the mantle of leadership is that when it comes to doing the right thing, there is no middle ground and there can be no equivocating. Little sins of omission have a nasty habit of growing into big sins of commission. A little fudging on an expense report is the same as digging into the corporate till with a big Caterpillar 972H wheel loader, and should be treated in the same manner.

LOSE THE LOSERS

People simply don't want to work for a leader who is dishonest, or one who tolerates dishonesty. Since the age of fifteen, my son has worked in the restaurant industry. His career has led him to positions in virtually every corporately owned casual-theme chain. At one point during his tenure with a well-known California-based concept, his store's management team learned that about one-third of their employees seemingly couldn't tell the difference between their money and the company's money—an all-too-common problem in a fast-paced, cash-intensive business.

> *People simply don't want to work for a leader who is dishonest, or one who tolerates dishonesty.*

The store's GM, in his infinite wisdom, awarded the thirty-some miscreants a verbal warning (yes, you read that correctly—verbal warning), on the logic that "if we terminate all of them, we won't be able to keep the doors open." The net result? A lot of their better employees immediately packed up and headed for the exits, muttering something about not having to work with thieves and losers. With a bright green light on for stealing, we hate to think what the rest of the workforce was soon up to.

> *If you stand up and be counted, from time to time you may get yourself knocked down. But remember this: A man flattened by an opponent can get up again. A man flattened by conformity stays down for good.* —Thomas J. Watson Jr., founder, IBM[4]

DO YOU MEASURE UP?

Following are ten characteristics that have a lot to do with the special trust that is vested in anyone who would occupy a leadership role, and a handful of self-test questions any leader (or aspirant) would do well to ask themselves.

1. **Am I TRUSTWORTHY?** Am I unfailingly, unflinchingly truthful? Do I keep my promises? Is honesty part of my very fiber? Can people depend on me to do what I've said I will do?

2. **Am I LOYAL?** Am I true to those around me—my family, friends, co-workers, the organization?

3. **Am I HELPFUL?** Am I concerned about other people? Am I apt to do things willingly for others, without reward or recognition? Do I do them when no one is looking?

4. **Am I FRIENDLY?** Am I a brother/sister to those around me? Am I out-going toward those whose ideas and customs differ from mine?

5. **Am I COURTEOUS?** Am I polite to everyone regardless of their station in life? Do I remember (and practice) lessons learned from my childhood about the importance of good manners?

6. **Am I KIND?** Do I treat others with consideration—as I want to be treated? Do I avoid hurting others unnecessarily?

7. **Am I OBEDIENT?** Is my behavior consistent with the rules of the community, and society at large? If I think these rules and laws are unfair, do I try to have them changed in an orderly manner, rather than disobey them?

8. **Am I CHEERFUL?** Do I look for the bright side of things? Do I cheerfully attend to tasks that come my way? Do I make reasonable attempts to make others happy?

9. **Am I THRIFTY?** Am I a good steward of time and property?

10. **Am I BRAVE?** Leadership is not about being unafraid. In fact, it is highly likely that leaders face considerably greater danger than do non-leaders, and thus experience greater levels of fear. That said, am I willing to face danger even when I *am* afraid? Do I have the courage to stand for what I think is right, even when it is unpopular or unpleasant?

A strong case can be made for the notion that each characteristic reflected in the above list represents a "critical success factor" for leaders; to wit, a passing score is needed on all of them, not just a comfortable majority.

So, how'd you do? Please be very honest with yourself right now. In fact, you may want to ask one or two people who know you well and who have the capacity to be bone-honest to validate your scores. If you can "green light" each of the questions, you have crossed an important threshold in meeting the tests of being a successful leader and, for that matter, a Boy Scout. You see, these items are not only essential qualities for leadership, they happen to derive from the Boy Scout Law.[5]

Leadership is not about being unafraid.

If you can't, however, you'd do well to give serious thought to what else you should be doing to earn a living. Though many aspects of becoming a leader can be taught, we're fairly certain that things like courage, trustworthiness, and being cheerful are part of our DNA . . . you've either got 'em or you don't. They can't be taught.

CHAPTER SUMMARY

1. Good leaders have a reliable moral compass and can be expected to consistently do what they believe to be the right thing, even in the face of pressure and the absence of guidelines.
2. Right is right, not "kinda, sorta" right.
3. Ethical breaches usually are built on the backbone of a bunch of "little one-off decisions."
4. The character-related qualities of leadership cannot be absorbed through learning. This is NOT a training issue.

MONDAY MORNING, 8AM

1. Resolve to make the character-related qualities of leadership an absolute job requirement for leaders at your place.

2. Resolve to be more vigilant in stopping the "little one-off" decisions that have a nasty habit of becoming big ethical issues. Tell people you're doing it, then do it.

3. Make sure that everyone on your team understands clearly what you stand for, and that there are certain things you cannot do and continue to work here—no matter what.

7

SHUT UP AND LISTEN!

If you care, you listen. . . . Now when I say listen, I don't mean that
stilted baloney that so many officers engage in, and stand up to an
enlisted man and say, "How old are you, son, where're you from,
how long you been here? Thank you very much." Next man. Yeah,
that's baloney, that's form, that's pose. . . . Well, I'm not talking
about that kind of stuff. I'm talking about listening—LISTENING!
Because a little soldier won't come out and tell you everything's
all wrong. He'll be a little hesitant. If you ask him if he's getting
along all right and he just shrugs, he's getting along lousy. If he's not
enthusiastic in his response, there's something wrong. You'd better
dig a little deeper. —General Melvin Zais, U.S. Army, ret.[1]

The first major news story of 2006 was that thirteen miners were trapped two miles underground in the Sago mine, owned by International Coal Group in Buckhannon, West Virginia. Many were glued to their TVs throughout the night of January 3, awaiting word of what was happening down below in a suffocating blackness that few of us can even imagine.

Around midnight, it was reported that the miners had been found alive. Families, government and company officials, the press, and millions who were watching on that early morning engaged in jubilant celebration, heralding what many called the first miracle of the new year.

Nearly three hours later, the joy gave way to crushing heartbreak when it was announced that the news was wrong . . . way wrong. In fact, only one miner, twenty-six-year-old Randal L. McCloy Jr., emerged alive. What happened? This wasn't the pundits prematurely declaring the winner of a political election based on faulty exit polls. How could somebody be so wrong about something so important?

The impediments to hearing, and to listening, were formidable. The oxygen masks covering the rescuers' faces and generating constant noise, garbled radio transmissions, helicopters flying overhead, engine sounds, and the anxiety and excitement of the crowd all contributed to the bad—simply wrong—communication. But perhaps nothing contributed to the accidental, though critical, inaccuracy more than the collective psyche of those on the ground. They desperately *wanted* to hear of survival. Perhaps they simply heard what they wanted—needed so badly—to hear.

Listening. On its surface, it seems so basic, so natural. We simply let the sound come into our ears; we record, for a brief moment, what comes in, and then we respond. Or not. For something that seems so simple, so natural, there has been a mighty body of literature written and spoken about it. Amazon.com can sell you any (or all) of more than a quarter *million* books with the word "listening" in the title! This is not a book on listening, but it *is* a chapter, albeit a brief one, about how listening affects the willingness of people to part with discretionary effort. So, please, for the next few pages, listen up.

Listening, by contrast, is a choice—a willful act. We have to actually do something to listen.

We established early on that people reserve their best effort for those they believe care about them as human beings. One of the most convincing ways to let someone know you care is to listen to them. Really listen.

> *Listening is a sign of respect.* —Thomas L. Friedman, columnist, *New York Times*[2]

While the words "hear" and "listen" are both verbs, the former is passive and the latter is active. Provided we have the physiology to support the sense of hearing, we hear a thing, whether we like it or not. Listening, by contrast, is a choice—a willful act. We have to actually *do* something to listen.

One of us, at the tender age of forty-three, was fitted with the latest in digital hearing aids to treat a hereditary early hearing loss. While his wife notices a marked improvement in his hearing, she says the $5,000 they spent on the devices didn't do much for his listening. Our willingness to listen seems to be driven, in part, by our perception of how valuable the information we're hearing is to us. In other words, if you really *need* or *want* the information you're hearing, you bet your boots you'll listen.

The opposite of listening is waiting to talk.

Imagine that you're on a flight and you've got an almost impossibly tight connection. (If you're accustomed to connecting through Atlanta, this will require little imagination on your part.) The flight attendant is reading off the list of connecting gates. The PA quality is Edisonian, and the person next to you is ripping off some clamorous, bourbon-induced snores—but you need to hear your connection information. This demonstrates what it means to *listen,* actively listen. Likewise, in emergencies or other episodes of stress, we somehow manage to find the ability to listen. Why, then, do we find it so difficult to listen to people in other situations, such as at work or at home?

The opposite of listening is waiting to talk. Perhaps one reason we so often fail at listening is because we excel at its opposite. There are several pairs (or groups) of activities that we, as humans, can perform simultaneously. It breaches the bounds of good taste to enumerate many of them. But just like sneezing while holding your eyes open, it is simply impossible to both speak and listen simultaneously. We would all do well to take the occasional look in the mirror, as a reminder that most of us were endowed with exactly one mouth, and double that ration of ears.

In one leadership training course we frequently lead—a course on having coaching discussions with people at work—we always ask, near the beginning of the seminar, for a list of attributes of people who are good at coaching. Between the two of us, we've led this course several hundred times, and we can say with near certainty that we have never, *never* asked that question when one of the responses was *not* "listening."

And yet, in this same seminar, when we record and then play back an initial coaching practice discussion, we often find that the person who is supposed to be doing the coaching has spent 75, 80, sometimes as much as 95 percent of the "air time" *talking.* Which means he or she can't *possibly* be listening.

Good leaders have developed the *habit* of listening. They've made it part of their nature. It's a strategy. Even if you think you're in the habit of listening most of the time, here are some specific instances when we, as leaders, really need to listen, but often fail to:

- **During interviews.** Here our tendency to hear what we want to hear, rather than listening, bites us, and bites us hard, with lasting implications.
- **When addressing the troops.** When interacting with a group of employees (or others), we commonly ask, "How's it going?" never stopping to listen to the answer, if there even is one. That's too bad, because the response can be telling. We would do well to allow (even encourage) the person to respond, and to discern between what we heard (e.g., "fine") and what we did NOT hear, as in even a scintilla of enthusiasm.
- **When it's your heart that's speaking.**

LISTEN ONE AT A TIME

In chapter 1, we introduced Command Sgt. Maj. Michele Jones, who was, until her retirement in 2006, the highest-ranking non-commissioned officer in the U.S. Army Reserve, and the first woman appointed to the role. I had the opportunity to talk at some length with her at a workforce development meeting for reservists, during which Jones and I had both been speakers.

Our conversation, held in the courtyard of the hotel where the meeting was taking place, was interrupted no fewer than a dozen times by grateful and respectful soldiers who just wanted to say a word of appreciation to Jones, both for her comments that morning and, in a larger sense, for what she had meant to them over the last few years.

In no way did I resent these interruptions. Indeed, I welcomed them. Those soldiers had first rights to speak to her. I was a visitor. And in those conversations with soldiers, I observed, firsthand, a demonstration of good listening.

In every instance, while Jones was speaking to a soldier, that soldier had the sergeant major's full attention. She was focused, 100 percent, on the person who was taking the time to speak with her. It didn't matter that she had been on the road for weeks, hadn't slept much the night before, had a broken foot, a meeting with a lieutenant colonel in an hour, four other soldiers standing in line to talk to her, and me sitting nearby on a bench, waiting to pepper her with a few more questions.

While every encounter with a soldier started with words of salute and admiration from the soldier, in every case, she turned the conversation to "How are *you* doing? I'm still gonna be around for a few more months. What can I do for *you* before I leave?" "Your baby doin' alright? How 'bout your wife? How's she doin' about this deployment comin' up?"

DOWN 'N DIRTY

Hearing Aids

1. **Be prepared.** Listening is hard work and takes practice. Clear the decks; be "in the moment."

2. **Quiet the mind.** In the same way that listening can't take place while you're talking, it doesn't happen when you're thinking about something else. Consciously put all those other thoughts, worries, and problems you're trying to solve on hold while you're listening to someone else. You can come back and pick them up later.

3. **Focus.** We all like to talk (brag?) about multitasking. This is one area where the concept is just plain useless. Focus on the person you are listening to, nothing more, period. To the degree that you can, schedule your listening-intensive activities into that portion of the day when you are most alert.

4. **Listen with your eyes.** That's right, many good listeners listen as much with their eyes (and other senses) as they do with their ears. What are the other person's facial gestures? What is their body language telling you? A good self-test is to try to remember the color of the other person's eyes.

5. **Listen with empathy.** We listen best when we listen for understanding. It helps to put yourself in the other person's shoes and try to appreciate not just what they are saying, but what they are feeling. You can't do that if you are being judgmental, or readying your response.

6. **Ask questions.** As with any good reporter, getting a full appreciation for what the other person is saying (or trying to say) necessitates the asking of questions, sometimes tough questions.

7. **Take notes.** More than just a symbol, taking notes actually serves to reinforce in your brain what the other person is saying.

8. **Play it back.** Don't leave the conversation until you've verbally summarized (not parroted) what you've just listened to.

CHAPTER SUMMARY

1. Listening is not easy, nor does it come naturally to most of us. It is a choice, a conscious act that we have to work hard at.
2. The opposite of listening is waiting to talk.
3. We were issued two ears and one mouth for a reason.
4. Good leaders have developed the *habit* of listening.
5. Listening and multitasking are mutually exclusive. Don't even try. Focus all your energy and senses on the person you are listening to.
6. To the degree that you can, schedule your listening-intensive activities into that portion of the day when you are most alert.

MONDAY MORNING, 8AM

1. Make a conscious effort to be more aware of other people's listening habits. One of the residual benefits is that you will also become more aware of your own tendencies. When you meet someone with particularly good listening skills, compliment them, and engage them in a conversation of what works for them in this area.

2. Resolve to become a better listener in interview situations. Steps to doing so include being more prepared from the outset, and consciously pausing for at least four seconds between the time the candidate's mouth shuts and yours opens.

No man ever listened himself out of a job.   —Calvin Coolidge

THE AUTHENTIC LEADER

A man's a man, for all that. —Robert Burns, Scottish poet

SOUTHWEST CHARLIE

A couple of years ago, while waiting to board a Southwest Airlines flight in my home airport, I looked up and saw a familiar face. At first, I wasn't sure why the face was familiar, but my brain (such as it is) told me that I knew him, so, by reflex, I said, "Hello." The guy was about my age; maybe he's an old high school friend, I thought. While my mouth was forming the word "Hello," the aforementioned brain informed me that this was not, in fact, an old high school friend, or anybody I knew at all, but Charlie Crist, the attorney general of Florida. As a former state senator and education commissioner, he looked familiar only because he was a public figure. He'd been in the news lately because of rumors that he had been considering a run for governor, a claim he had so far refused to comment on. But the greeting had already commenced. I had to follow through, so I finished the sentence that began with "Hello" by adding, "Mr. Crist."

"It's just Charlie," he said. "How are you?" I introduced myself, and we— along with a guy from Kentucky—chatted for a half-hour or so, as you do with strangers you happen to sit next to in an airport. If Charlie's intention had been politicking, he was doing a lousy job. He spent all of his waiting time talking with the two of us. Even though I *do* live in Florida, I vote only once per election. So the maximum potential votes in play here was one.

This guy had been in public life for years, but the abiding impression I had of him after a few minutes was that Florida's attorney general was a regular guy. We exchanged business cards (his was, unlike mine, free from any cow images), and he wished me a pleasant trip as we boarded the jet.

About three months later, I happened to be attending the inauguration of John Delaney, the president of the University of North Florida. Waiting in line to enter the auditorium, I turned around, and there was my old friend, Charlie. He greeted me by my first name and said, "Contented Cows, right? Good to see you again. How've you been? Traveling much lately?"

Now, maybe this was just the smooth operation of a politician who, between the time of our airport meeting and President Delaney's inauguration, had confirmed those earlier rumors of a gubernatorial campaign for 2006.* But the fact that he was "just Charlie"; he had been flying on a $79 Southwest ticket (with his six foot three inch frame squeezed into a center seat); he remembered my name and something from my business card; and he was standing in line with the rest of us peons caused me to classify him a little differently from other politicians I knew. Ultimately, "Southwest Charlie's" demeanor caused me to give his candidacy more consideration than I might otherwise have done. He may be a politician, but to me at least, he seemed to be authentic, and thus, got the benefit of the doubt.

DR. BOZO

By contrast, one morning, while a client named Ellen and I were welcoming managers before the start of a leadership seminar at a hospital, a young man in a white coat walked into the meeting room and said, "What's going on in here? We're supposed to be having the daily patient update in here right now!" He was a young resident (are there any old residents?), not an adherent to the Dale Carnegie school of how to win friends and influence people, and apparently fond of throwing his new-found weight around.

Three days before, Ellen, a training manager for the hospital, had changed (and announced) meeting room assignments, owing to a schedule conflict and the ever-increasing demand for the hospital's limited meeting space.

---

*Charlie Crist was elected governor of Florida on November 7, 2006.

Ellen had e-mailed everyone involved, including the good doctor, but he had neglected to check his e-mail since then.

"You don't have the *authority* to change the room!" he barked to Ellen, whom he had never met before.

"Actually, doctor, I do. And I sent an e-mail letting you and the others know about it. I'm sorry if you didn't receive it," she responded, respectfully.

"I'm too busy to go around checking e-mails all the time!" he snarled.

Ellen gently directed him the twenty steps up the hall to the (much nicer) room to which his meeting had been reaccommodated. While she was away, most of the participants in the class, many of whom were nurse managers, made a note of the resident's name. One said, "Well, I know whose floor *not* to sign up for."

I only hoped this pompous and arrogant doctor treated his patients with more respect than he did his co-workers. He's the type who, unfortunately, gives his profession a reputation it doesn't wholly deserve. And he was already sending out signals likely to thwart—or at the very least, redirect—the discretionary effort of some of the nurses who might work with him at some point.

It calls for no great insight to recognize that the doctor's bad behavior was inappropriate, rude, and as we say in the south, tacky. But it probably serves as a good reminder that even those of us who *know* this isn't the way to play with others occasionally (like when we're under stress, which may be a lot of the time) pull rank (real or imagined) in order to get our way. Authentic leaders are careful to do better than that.

There's just something about knowing that our bosses, managers, doctors, and public servants are nothing more than regular people—and that *they* know it—that makes us want to give just a little bit more. It's what we call authenticity.

What makes an authentic leader? Here are some of the attributes that distinguish great leaders as authentic—the real deal—and which engender Oomph! from those they lead.

ATTRIBUTES OF THE AUTHENTIC LEADER

The first and most defining attribute of authentic leaders is that they are just plain folks. They work hard at keeping the air pressure inside their head equalized with the outside world. Or so it appears. And that's better than some well-known business leaders, politicians, entertainment figures—and, we're sorry to say, a few professional speakers and consultants—try to do.

Fred Smith, founder, CEO, and chairman of FedEx, and arguably the most successful businessperson in the state of Tennessee, will *never* walk through a doorway ahead of anyone else. He'll open the door and, without regard to gender, issue a humble "after you" gesture, and then follow. Part of this is just good upbringing. His mama raised him right. But part of it is authenticity. He knows he's smart, rich, and powerful, but more important, he knows he still puts his pants on the way everyone else does.

The first and most defining attribute of authentic leaders is that they are just plain folks.

On the other end of the scale, former Tyco executive Dennis Koslowski made no pretense of being a regular guy. According to court documents from his famed corruption trial, he was accused of spending a million of Tyco's dollars on a birthday bash for his second (and now former) wife Karen, in Sardinia, complete with costumed Roman gladiators and an ice sculpture of Michelangelo's David spraying vodka from . . . well, uh, it wasn't his mouth. "Koz," as he was unaffectionately known, is also alleged to have plundered the company coffers to set himself up in plush apartments and vacation villas filled with such accessories as a $15,000 umbrella stand in the shape of a poodle.

> *I'd rather have a guy who is a man of character than a bunch of characters.* —Jon Bon Jovi, rocker and owner of arena football team Philadelphia Soul

BOB HARVEY

Transcription Relief Services (TRS) of Greensboro, North Carolina, was the creation of Mary Harvey. The company grew quickly under Mary's leadership and earned a reputation as a haven for professional medical transcriptionists (MTs) to do work they enjoyed and to be treated with the respect that had seemingly eluded others in the field.

After Mary's death in 1999, her husband, Bob, the newly widowed father of young children, left his management job in the office products business and took over TRS. According to Kathy Rockel, the company's vice president whom we introduced in chapter 2, Bob's favorite saying is "Before honor comes humility."

DOWN 'N DIRTY

Authentic Leaders

Being authentic isn't a program. You can't fake it. It is who you are. But you can change some of your personal habits. Authentic leaders:

1. Welcome others' points of view—it's OK to disagree with them. They don't "shoot the messenger."
2. Know that being real is as important as being right.
3. Have no qualms about saying, "I don't know."
4. Are reliably honest, open, and transparent . . . WYSIWYG.
5. Regularly build up those around them. Giving heartfelt "atta-boys" and sharing credit is a well-practiced habit for them.
6. Are as considerate to the shoeshine guy or a restaurant server as to a member of their country club.
7. Aren't afraid to admit they've screwed up, and to apologize.
8. Roll up their sleeves.

"I don't know anyone who cares more than Bob does," Kathy told us, "and he's consistently pushing *us* to care, and to show it."

TRS employs about eighty-five home-based MTs across forty or so states, many in the nation's snow belt. One recent winter, a transcriptionist's furnace gave up the ghost. Bob knew that this particular MT wasn't in a position to replace it, and he knew why. So he bought her a new one. He didn't make a big deal of it; he just took care of it so that her house (where, by the way, she did all her work) would be warm.

And in 2006, when his family—this time his work family—was again struck by tragedy, his reflex response was to cover the situation with caring. While he and his employees were all returning to their various home locations from the company's 2006 annual meeting in the Tennessee mountains, one of TRS's transcription managers, a woman named Regina, received the news that her teenage son had been critically injured in a car accident. "It was then that I knew that Bob really saw us as an extended family," Kathy Rockel said.

Bob got on the horn and tried to find someone who could divert their trip home to drive to Kentucky to be with Regina and her family. A co-worker named Melissa, who lived in another state, volunteered. "Fill up your car with gas," Bob told her, "and send me your expenses when you get home." The young man died three days later.

At the same time, the company had customers to serve and something of a planned backlog due to the company meeting. Bob had customer commitments that he felt he couldn't break, but he made sure the company was well-represented at the funeral.

Then, remembering how he had felt after losing his wife, he said, "We need people to go down there next week. It's the week *after* that's the hardest." And during "the week after," Bob left a meeting in Illinois, drove to Kentucky, and spent time with Regina and her family.

Kathy said, "No matter what, Bob wants to make sure everyone is taken care of as well as they can be. And we have some of the hardest working people I've ever seen, because of that."

Not only is Bob Harvey kind and caring, as an authentic leader, he welcomes—no, encourages—people to disagree with him. He knows he certainly doesn't know everything there is to know about his business and, in fact, thinks it's his people's job to tell him when he's wrong. Authentic leaders build up the confidence of those around them. They're self-confident, but not grand or arrogant.

Authentic leaders build up the confidence of those around them. They're self-confident, but not grand or arrogant.

Ainslee Tyree, TRS's human resources manager, told us, "Everybody 'loses it' (their temper, their composure) from time to time. Bob's no exception. But when he does, he always goes to each person he 'lost it at,' and apologizes." That takes courage . . . and authenticity.

Authentic leaders are transparent and approachable. What you see is what there is. Bob Harvey challenges his people to live the values they talk about. One of those values is having the integrity to walk away from business they don't believe they can do well. Some leaders sell a job, and then hope their people can figure out how to deliver. Bob encourages TRS people to stretch and take challenges, but he'll never knowingly put them in a position where he doesn't really believe they'll be able to succeed.

COMMAND SERGEANT MAJOR MICHELE JONES

The setting was a ballroom at the Ponce Hilton on the south coast of Puerto Rico. I had been invited to speak for the Annual Workforce Retention

Symposium of the 65th Regional Readiness Command, United States Army Reserve, which is stationed on the island. These were Puerto Rican soldiers and officers, not a mainland unit on a jaunt to the Caribbean. I was in the unenviable position on the program of following Command Sgt. Maj. Michele Jones, whose listening skills we described in the previous chapter. Unenviable because the audience didn't know me, and they knew CSM Jones. Not only did they know her, they respected, admired, and—I would even say—revered this uncommon leader.

A frequent visitor to the island and to this unit, and a regular speaker at this annual event, Jones, a mainlander from Baltimore, Maryland, with self-described OFS (over-forty syndrome), had developed a tradition of doing a little salsa (the dance, not the condiment) on stage, as a respectful tip-of-the-hat to the island's culture. And maybe also to show them that the highest-ranking NCO in the Army Reserve wasn't afraid to show her human side. This time, in August of 2006, she took the stage sporting a soft cast on her right foot, placed there by an Army surgeon just weeks before, to hold the foot together after a fracture.

When the audience saw the casted foot, their first reaction was "What? No salsa?!" Then, the catchy music filled the room, a predesignated officer joined her onstage, and the two rocked the room with a brief and safety-modified version of the dance that everyone there had come to associate with Michele Jones.

While the dance definitely put a glow into the room, it was nothing compared to her dialogue with (not speech to) the audience. Jones's distinction as a leader has less to do with where she's been and what she's accomplished (and believe me, it's impressive) than who she is in the eyes of the soldiers under her command. She possesses that rare ability to commingle "tough as nails" with "gracious." She's no softie. No pushover. But she cares about soldiers.

"If you're an overweight soldier, I'm gonna tell you about it. And I may not be too nice about it when I tell you," she told me. "But I'm not telling you that to hurt your feelings. This isn't about looking cute in your uniform. No, sir. I'm not making a fashion statement here. This is about being able to carry your battle buddy maybe a long way to get medical attention. It's about your battle buddy being able to carry *you*. And he's not leaving you behind. So if he can't pick you up 'cause you enjoyed too many meals a little too much, that might get both of you killed, and I'm not having that if I can help it."

The only downer in the room was the fact that everyone there knew that Sgt. Maj. Jones had announced her retirement, and that this would be her last visit to Puerto Rico as a member of the military. Later that afternoon, after both of us had spoken, we sat down in the courtyard of the hotel's meeting area, and she talked with me about leadership, service, caring, and, of course, discretionary effort.

During our courtyard visit, one young soldier approached Jones and started by saying, "Ma'am, I just want to salute you. Thank you for what you said this morning." Then he commented, respectfully, on the fact that there was a certain designation that he knew she had earned, as had he, but that she wasn't wearing on her battle uniform. This was something she was entitled, but not required, to wear.

She said, "That's just a choice I've made. I don't want to take anything away from anyone who's earned this. It's just that when I'm in this uniform [the battle uniform], I choose to keep it clean . . . keep it simple."

When we returned to the bench where we were sitting, she told me more. That she chose not to wear the designation on her battle uniform because she wanted to be approachable. "I never want a soldier to think 'I really shouldn't talk to her. Look at all those things on her uniform.' Some soldiers might do that. I hope it doesn't come across as false modesty, but I have to stay approachable. Otherwise, what am I doing here?"

> *Be more concerned with your character than your reputation, because your character is what you really are, while your reputation is merely what others think you are.* —John Wooden, basketball coach

CHAPTER SUMMARY

1. The first and most defining attribute of authentic leaders is that they are just plain folks.
2. Being authentic isn't a program. You can't fake it. It is who you are. But you can change some of your personal habits.
3. It is as important to be real as to be right.
4. Authentic leaders aren't afraid of saying, "I don't know" or "I screwed up."
5. Authentic leaders are transparent and approachable. WYSIWYG.
6. Authentic leaders are as considerate to the shoeshine guy or a restaurant server as to a member of their country club.
7. Authentic leaders are self-confident, but not grand or arrogant.

MONDAY MORNING, 8am

1. Conduct a quick examination of personal habits that "separate" you unnecessarily from the people on your team. Look for areas where you expect (or just get) undue deference, or for things that serve to remind everyone who the boss is.

2. Get in the habit of being more of a servant leader with your team. Clean up the break room (if you're not in the habit of doing that anyway). Cook a meal, bring it in, serve it to your team, and then clean up afterwards. Perform some act of hospitality to demonstrate that you lead them best by serving. Sadly, many managers believe that showing their human side in the workplace reflects weakness—that's a crock.

3. Make it a practice to go above and beyond expectations when someone on your team experiences a personal loss or tragedy. There's no formula, no model here. Just do what you'd do if it were a member of your own family. The return will be exponential.

4. Convene a team meeting, and challenge the group to tell you something that you're just flat wrong about. Some idea, notion, assumption that you think is golden, but that they know is bunk. Set ground rules that include respectfulness, truth, honesty, and constructiveness. Then, reward the best, boldest, and most courageous challenge you receive.

9

MOTIVATION THROUGH MISSION

*Leaders are visionaries with a poorly developed sense of
fear and no concept of the odds against them. They make
the impossible happen.* —Dr. Robert Jarvik, inventor

On September 12, 1962, President John F. Kennedy stood in the hot Texas
sun at Houston's Rice University stadium and, in a short, 2,205-word speech,
announced clearly and forcefully that the United States had joined the "space
race." Picking up a gauntlet thrown down by the Soviet Union, Kennedy
committed the nation to a path of exploration and scientific achievement of
epic proportions.

We would be the first nation to successfully send explorers to the moon
(and bring them back), and we would do it before the end of the decade. To
put this challenge in perspective, one only need recall that it occurred four
years before full network production of color television programming in the
United States!

> But if I were to say, my fellow citizens, that we shall send to the
> moon, 240,000 miles away from the control station in Houston,
> a giant rocket more than three hundred feet tall . . . made of new
> metal alloys, some of which have not yet been invented, capable of
> standing heat and stresses several times more than have ever been
> experienced, fitted together with a precision better than the finest
> watch, carrying all the equipment needed for propulsion, guidance,

control, communications, food and survival, on an untried mission, to an unknown celestial body, and then return it safely to earth, re-entering the atmosphere at speeds of over 25,000 miles per hour, causing heat about half that of the temperature of the sun—almost as hot as it is here today—and do all this, and do it right, and do it first before this decade is out—*then we must be bold.*[1]

Kennedy's speech and the announced objective created a unifying sense of purpose the likes of which America had not experienced in some time. His remarks, and the objective itself, were bold, clear, and compelling. We were going to do something that had never been done, or even seriously contemplated. Americans got the not-so-subtle hint that losing this race to the Russians, our declared enemy, would not be a good thing for the national interest. No doubt many ventured outside that evening, and many evenings thereafter, and glanced upward to the sky at the big white shiny reminder of our collective national task.

The Apollo Space Program arose as a result of Kennedy's initiative, causing many to do a lot more than just look at the moon a little differently. Fully engaged by the bold challenge, NASA's 36,000 employees, together with some 376,700 federal contractors, including some of the world's pre-eminent physicists, metallurgists, medical specialists, pilots, engineers, and other specialists, did the very best work of their lives in order to accomplish the mission.

And accomplish it they did. On July 24, 1969, Americans everywhere held their breath as astronauts Neil Armstrong, Buzz Aldrin, Michael Collins, and the Apollo 11 spacecraft safely returned to earth after planting an American flag on the lunar surface.

Despite incredibly long odds and serious adversity—including a 1967 launch pad accident that killed three astronauts, the Vietnam War, and the death of President Kennedy—the Apollo Program had survived and the mission had been accomplished. A good part of the success can be attributed to the fact that, by painting (and then vigorously reinforcing) a picture that was bold, graphic, and compelling, Kennedy had set in motion what became a national sense of mission.

Though Americans continue to venture into space, the results since that moment have been far less compelling. Why? Perhaps the answer can be best found via some field research. Go ask a half-dozen people from various walks of life what the "mission" of America's space program is. For that matter, ask an equal number of NASA employees. Take a tour of NASA's Web site or read some of the literature and see if you can discover it. Ask a couple of your elected representatives, who appropriate the agency's funding.

Our bet is that the responses will resemble a completely dumbfounded, "deer-in-the-headlights" expression. The inescapable conclusion is that we don't *have* a clear, compelling sense of purpose and direction for our space program, ergo we're having a very difficult time gaining traction.

Whether for good or evil purposes, having a sense of purpose is a powerful motivator indeed.

MISSION FOR THE DEVIL

Thirty-nine years, almost to the day, after President Kennedy's Rice University speech, the world was reminded just how compelling a sense of purpose can be, as nineteen men commandeered four commercial airliners and flew three of them into U.S. landmarks and one into the Pennsylvania countryside, killing more than 2,700 innocent people in the most deadly foreign attack ever on American soil.

According to Terry McDermott in *Perfect Soldiers,* these "were, regrettably, I think, fairly ordinary men. I say this is regrettable because it was their ordinariness that makes it much more likely there are a great many more men just like them. In the end, then, this is a story about the power of belief to remake ordinary men; it is a story about the dangerous power of ideas wrongly wielded."[2]

Ordinary or not, on a mission sponsored by Islamic extremists, masterminded and financed by Osama bin Laden, and carried out by his al Qaeda organization, the 9/11 hijackers were utterly convinced that they were on a mission from God, a mission that warranted their own suicide, and that would earn them a place in heaven. Whether for good or evil purposes, having a sense of purpose is a powerful motivator indeed.

WE WILL NOT FALTER AND WE WILL NOT FAIL

Three days after the 9/11 attack, President George W. Bush stood at the still-smoldering ruins of the World Trade Center in New York to witness the devastation firsthand and pay tribute to the firefighters and other rescue workers who were still digging through the rubble in hopes of finding survivors.

Struggling to be heard over the din of the city, Bush borrowed a bullhorn from a firefighter and announced, "I can hear you. The rest of the world hears you, and the people who knocked these buildings down will hear all of us soon." Not exactly known as a skilled orator, Bush nonetheless connected at that moment with a nervous nation, and indeed the world.

The hunt was on. We were on a mission to identify and neutralize any individual, state, or nation that had anything to do with this terrorist act, and to take steps to prevent its recurrence.

The terrorist acts of that late summer day galvanized the people of the United States as had no other single event since the bombing of Pearl Harbor sixty years before. America, and indeed most of the world, was single-mindedly determined to show, by their actions, solidarity behind President Bush's statement that such acts "will not stand." But it was much more than rhetoric. America (indeed all free nations) had been attacked, evoking a more sustained, concerted reaction than had been seen in a half-century.

An early manifestation of this solidarity—this commitment to mission—was demonstrated in the reconstruction project at the Pentagon, a large portion of which had been destroyed in the attack when it was hit by American Airlines flight #77. Code-named the "Phoenix Project" (as in from the ashes), the work commenced almost immediately, on September 29.

"We want to have people back in the building on E Ring, where the aircraft impacted, by September 11 [of 2002]," declared Lee Evey, the government's Phoenix Project manager. "We want them to be sitting at their desks performing their mission. Everyone associated with the project wants to bring the building back as quickly as possible. That's our goal. And that's our mission."

Easy to understand. Clear. Compelling.

A large countdown clock with red numbers reflecting the hours and minutes remaining until the deadline served as an ever-present reminder of the mission. As if any additional impetus were really needed, the clock also bore the words "Let's Roll," in tribute to those who bravely defended the city by bringing down the fourth hijacked jet before it could reach its target.

Visual. Graphic. Visceral. Precise.

Early on, crews toiled around the clock, completing demolition work projected to take eight months in only thirty-one days, in a feat that would set the pace for the rest of the endeavor. Much of the interior structure was rebuilt that winter. Between February 25 and June 11, more than four thousand pieces of limestone were installed on the building's facade. April 5 was the last day of concrete work.

In the early stages of the project, as many as one thousand workers labored throttle-up, with heart and soul, in three eight-hour shifts a day. As work progressed, the required workforce dropped to an average of about six hundred. Evey cut back the schedule to two ten-hour

When people are truly committed—hell-bent, "bound and determined"—to do something, almost no obstacle and no degree of inconvenience or difficulty can deter them.

shifts a day, six days a week. "We didn't want to continue to push these guys seven days a week, twenty-four hours a day, because we were concerned that we could start to have accidents on the job," he said. Even at the 24/7 pace, the safety record was astounding. After more than 860,000 worker-hours on the job, there had been only one lost-time accident, a minor thumb injury.

At Christmas, Evey insisted that all the workers take two days off. A group of sixty-four objected, saying they wanted to work straight through.[3]

When people are truly committed—hell-bent, "bound and determined"— to do something, almost no obstacle and no degree of inconvenience or difficulty can deter them. They're oblivious to the personal sacrifices required—at least for a time—in pursuit of a meaningful mission.

Phoenix Project workers gladly worked hours that would probably have produced much bellyaching had the work been for yet another office building along Northern Virginia's Dulles corridor, just a few miles away. They put up with Washington's winter weather. They endured disruptions in the regular flow of their lives. Some chose to forego longer, more lucrative jobs. Many missed holiday festivities, kids' soccer games, and the chance to sleep late on weekends. But it didn't matter.

Michael Bratti, whose company performed much of the stonework for the project, told *Masonry Construction* magazine, "Everyone had an attitude of 'Get it done.' No one complained. Everyone was eager to do what they could out of a personal sense of duty. We all realized what a once-in-a-lifetime opportunity this was for us."[4]

During a Pentagon press briefing on June 11, 2002, project manager Lee Evey was asked to comment on the extraordinary dispatch with which the project had progressed. He said:

Believe me, you will not probably ever step foot on another construction project in your life that has people as motivated as the people are on that project right now. People don't really pay that much attention to what their title is, what their job is, and what they've been specifically told to do. They pitch in, they work, they help, they support one another, and it's been very, very effective.

We've attempted to set very clear goals, set forth the work in a very clear manner, so that people understand exactly what it is that's required of them, and we have as little lost time and [as much] work accomplished . . . as possible.[5]

As hoped, on the first anniversary of 9/11, the work *was* completed, and the offices that had been vaporized a year before were back in service. The fact that a government construction project of that magnitude was completed within one year might be surprising enough to many, until they learn that the entire building was built in a span of just 422 days, after the U.S. was attacked in Hawaii and joined the Second World War. Perhaps that, too, says something about the motivating power of mission. But what strikes us about the 2001–2002 restoration of the Pentagon has more to do with who started and finished the job than with the efficiency of the endeavor.

Data from the U.S. Labor Department's Bureau of Labor Statistics at the time showed that the annual employee turnover rate on projects like this one could be expected to be around 25 percent. And yet the employee turnover rate on this project was practically nil. Zero. The big goose egg. For all intents and purposes, every person—employed by the dozens of contractors working on the job—who started the project saw it through to completion.

Gen. Richard Myers, then-chairman of the Joint Chiefs of Staff, paid tribute to the builders, calling them "hard-hat patriots." Myers said, "With muscle, determination, marble, cement, and Indiana limestone, you did more than repair our windows and walls, you repaired our souls."[6]

THIS IS A FOOTBALL

Legend has it that one day shortly after signing on as head coach of the Green Bay Packers in 1958, Vince Lombardi whistled practice to a halt, assembled his players—who had grown way too accustomed to losing—and got instructive about the organization's goals, roles, mission, and rules. He began with the statement, "This is a football."

Indulge us, please, while we rant for a minute. When it comes to defining our organization's mission, this is an area where most of us manager-types have just plain done a miserable job. Now, when we say "organization," we're not referring only to the corporation, agency, university, or other entity whose logo appears on your paycheck; we also mean your department, store, restaurant, team, office, perhaps even just your own cubicle—that entity over which you have the greatest influence. Is there mission clarity there? How do we create it and sustain it? Does any of this matter? And where have we gone wrong?

We have managed to thoroughly confuse and mislead people about why the organization exists, and where it's headed.

Even worse than failing to communicate with our workforce about the organization's ultimate ambition and direction, we have managed to thoroughly confuse and mislead people about why the organization exists, and where it's headed. How? By allowing well-intentioned but misguided folk to turn what once may have been a pretty clear signal about the organization's most important priorities into a raft of slogans, banners, buzzwords, t-shirts, and wall plaques—"mission flatulence" if you will. That's right—hype, noise.

If you at all doubt what we're saying, start taking note of all the plaques and banners proclaiming a "mission" you see when you enter a place of business—any business. Do it at your own business. Notice how formulaic many of these mission statements have become. It's almost as though some high-priced consultant cut a swath through the corporate world a few years ago, purveying a boilerplate for a fortune-changing mission statement for all who would but fill in the blanks.

_____ will be (future tense compulsory; avoid
[Company Name]
weasel words like "try" or even "endeavor") the world's preeminent provider

of market-based _____ solutions (mis-
[industry or type of service or product]
sion statements without the word "solutions" will not be accepted) serving

_____ through a commitment to _____
[customers, markets, or other constituency]
_____, _____, and _____.
[three lofty ideals espoused by CEO, picked up during golf game with competitor]

Think we're exaggerating about mission flatulence? Check out your own closet, and pull out all those promotional T-shirts proclaiming "job 1," "mission 1," what your team stands for, and the like. Bet you've got enough stuff there to clothe a small town.

In essence, what we've done is confuse a mission statement (something anybody with a sixth-grade education can create in less than five minutes) with a "sense of mission," something that can require an entire lifetime of daily reinforcement.

Entire lifetime?! Why bother? Because, as we have already established (we hope), having a sense of mission to which one is absolutely committed is an extremely powerful motivator. Without it, people are just along for the ride.

In his 1986 book, *Peak Performers,* Charles Garfield did a masterful job of explaining how "motivation through mission" has worked for astronauts, Olympic athletes, and—yes—regular folks. Every single instance of high achievement in the history of mankind has been accompanied by someone being committed (in a big way) to a mission![7]

Every single instance of high achievement in the history of mankind has been accompanied by someone being committed (in a big way) to a mission!

What else could have caused astronaut Alan Shepard to strap his butt to a relatively untested rocket, Christopher Columbus to sail off the edge of the known earth, or Martin Luther King Jr. to march into Selma, Alabama? It sure wasn't the pay!

Moreover, what else could have caused eight million Iraqis, in January of 2005, to risk death at the hands of Zarqawi-led bullies by visibly going into a polling place, voting, and then smearing purple ink on their hand to prove that they had done so?

WHAT'S COMING OUT OF YOUR HORN?

The late jazz saxophonist Charlie "Bird" Parker once said of music, "If you don't live it, it won't come out of your horn." So, what's coming out of *your* horn?

Often, when speaking at a corporate event or conducting a training session, we'll see one of the aforementioned banners, plaques, or posters proclaiming the company's mission. Do you think their people can recite the mission statement? Who cares? Here's what we think is a better barometer of your success in creating a sense of mission. We've issued the following challenge to many clients, and extend the same to you.

For the next class of new recruits you bring in, shield them from any verbal manifestations of the esteemed "mission statement." Make darn sure none of their eyes or ears comes in contact with its words, from any source, for a period of three months. At the end of that time, after they've had a chance to get to know your company and its leaders, ask them, "What is this company—this place—all about?" Their answer will tell you all you need to know.

So, you ask, what are the essentials of motivation through mission, and where are the "better practices"—who is getting it right?

CLARITY

In its earliest days, FedEx—or Federal Express as it was known then—didn't have a lot going for it. The company had precious little money. It wasn't uncommon to have the electricity turned off in a field station due to an unpaid utility bill or to have an asset seized for back taxes. They had even less time. And, as an early proponent of airline deregulation, they certainly didn't have many friends.

What they did have, though, was a couple thousand people with a warrior spirit who would rather fall on their swords than be responsible for missing a commitment to a customer.

The FedEx example bears mentioning because it illustrates one of the essential ingredients of achieving a true sense of mission . . . *clarity.* They hadn't declared that they would "try" to do something, or that something was "job 1" or "priority 1." There was no ambiguity or "wiggle room" to it whatsoever. No, what had been spoken and accepted was this notion that, against some very long odds, they were going to do something that no one else at the time was capable of doing, namely pick your stuff up today and deliver it somewhere else absolutely, positively overnight—no matter what.

BOLDNESS

On the premise that modest achievement isn't terribly energizing or memorable, a mission must also be bold if it is to inspire peak performance. To be sure, we can't all commit the nation to a successful lunar mission as President

Kennedy did in 1962, or predict Superbowl victories like former NFL coach Jimmy Johnson, but if we are to inspire greatness, we must somehow get people to "hitch their wagon" to something big—credible, but big, bold, graphic, and compelling.

THE NEED FOR AN OPPONENT

While "enemy" may be too strong a word, the presence of an opponent, adversary, or clear and present danger seems to have a lot to do with the level of conviction that accompanies a sense of purpose or mission. If nothing else, the presence of an opposing force concentrates the mind and allows us to focus.

In his paper, "What Does It Mean To Be a USNA Graduate?" George P. Watts Jr., president of the United States Naval Academy Alumni Association, contrasted the impact of having (versus not having) an opponent, using the Naval Academy classes of 1943, 1973, and 2003 as examples. He noted that, not unlike the '43 class, which graduated into the teeth of a world war, his own (1973) class, immediately upon graduation, served with a clear mission against a known adversary in a cold war.

About the class of 2003, however, he said, "These midshipmen face a world that is, in many ways, much more complex, much more challenging, and much more dangerous. They do not have the clarity of mission nor adversary that we in the classes of '43 and '73 were afforded. We left Bancroft Hall sure of who the enemy was and assuming that the fight would be somewhat fair; that is, fought using some sort of rules or established doctrine. As the men and women of today's Naval Academy graduate and are commissioned in the Navy and Marine Corps, they will face a much different and complex world than we did just a 'short' thirty years ago."[8]

One wonders how resolute and successful the United States would have been in the Apollo Program were it not for the Russian space program and the fact that they had established a clear lead in space exploration. Or, had Osama bin Laden not succeeded in his 9/11 attack, how long would it have taken to complete a building project like the Pentagon renovation?

FedEx's Fred Smith put it very succinctly, "If UPS weren't around, we would have had to invent them."

A SENSE OF MISSION CAN BE FRAGILE

On May 1, 2003, in a well-publicized photo op, President George W. Bush made a landing aboard the USS *Abraham Lincoln* in a Navy S-3B Viking jet. The purpose of the trip was ostensibly to welcome the *Lincoln's* sailors and airmen back from a tour in the Persian Gulf.

Later that afternoon, as the president addressed the nation from the carrier deck, advising the world that major combat operations in Iraq had been concluded, he had the misfortune to be photographed standing in front of a giant banner that read, "Mission Accomplished." The banner didn't say, "Great Job," "Welcome Home," "We're Proud of You," or any such thing, but rather, "Mission Accomplished." Given the linkage that had been strongly suggested between the War on Terror and the War in Iraq, our sense of purpose began to falter almost immediately.

Within days, America and indeed the rest of the world began to draw deeper and more assured breaths as the spotlight was moved onto other things. We thought we were done and so, in this country, the very cause that had bound us seemed settled. As a result, our newfound sense of unity began to unravel and, within a few short months, we entered a "red state-blue state" tug-of-war unlike anything the United States had seen since the 1860s.

Note: Our interest in this example has nothing whatsoever to do with the politics of the matter, but rather it serves as an excellent reminder of the fragile nature of a sense of purpose and direction. Absent active care, feeding, and support, the light on the cause burns less brightly with each passing day, until one day when the lamp just goes out.

CHAPTER SUMMARY

1. Whether for good or evil purposes, a sense of purpose and direction is a powerful motivator.
2. A mission must be clear, bold, consistent, and simple.
3. A sense of mission needs an opponent almost as much as it needs an advocate.
4. A sense of mission can be fragile.
5. To be engaging, a mission must be visceral, graphic, and precise. Think 9/11, Project Phoenix (Pentagon reconstruction), the countdown clock with big red numbers, and the words "Let's Roll."

MONDAY MORNING, 8AM

1. Right now, write down what you believe to be your organization's raison d'etre and top three business priorities.

2. Next, go ask the same question of the first five or six people you see at work. If you're a manager, ask people on your team.

3. Compare their responses, and then compare them to your answer. Next, ask your boss the same question.

4. If everyone in your workgroup had a consistent understanding of your organization's "mission," what would the impact be on your business? Your customers? Each other?

5. List three things you can do *routinely* that would improve the understanding and the execution of your organization's mission on the part of those you work with.

SECTION THREE

THE OOMPH! ENVIRONMENT

CHAPTER
10

TRUST

Making commitments generates hope. Keeping commitments generates trust. —Blaine Lee, founding vice president, FranklinCovey

Anyone who has attended a Cirque du Soleil show has witnessed an incredible display of talent and timing, and one of the central lubricants of Oomph! At any given point, one or more of the performers are hurtling through the air, high above the stage, unprotected by nets or safety devices, relying on fellow performers to catch them before they plunge to the floor below, with certain injury as a result.

In another world, that of high-performance automobile racing, Indy (and their counterpart, NASCAR) drivers tear around asphalt tracks at speeds in excess of 200 mph, at times only fractions of an inch away from speedway walls and other cars. At that speed, the failure of any component of the vehicle itself, a crew member, or another driver could result in a fireball, an ugly pile of fiberglass shards, twisted metal, and death.

What enables Cirque's performers and the Andrettis and Gordons of the world to do what they do? Hint: It's a "t" word—big time, capital "T"—*Trust*. Trust that the woman who rigged the trapeze did her job, that the pit crew got all the lug nuts tight on the last tire change, that management didn't scrimp on cheap brake pads, that the guy who is supposed to catch you in midair doesn't sneeze at the wrong time, and yes—trust in your own instincts and abilities.

LOWER AND SLOWER

Absent that trust, it's safe to say that these folks would be doing their thing a lot lower and slower. Absent that kind of trust, it's also safe to say that your people are doing something other than Oomphing. Trust is an omnipresent element in any high-performance team where humans are at work or play. Trust that I'm not going to get hurt or screwed, trust that people are going to do what they say they will, and trust that when push comes to shove, we'll all be rowing in the same direction.

Not unlike the character-based leadership qualities mentioned in chapter 6, the degree of trust required to really go flat-out is absolute. People have to lay it all out in order to perform at their full potential and not spend one nanosecond wondering if the guy down the hall in marketing has a surreptitious agenda, or if the HR representative can competently screen résumés for a new position vacancy.

> *The degree of trust required to really go flat-out is absolute.*

A 2005 report by BlessingWhite, Inc., dealt with the impact of trust on workplace engagement, defined by the firm as "the alignment of maximum job satisfaction with maximum job contribution." The survey upon which the report is based suggests the existence of a "significant connection between plans to stay or leave (one's job) and trust in one's manager." Indeed, of those respondents expressing intent to leave their employer, 37 percent said they didn't trust their managers. By contrast, of those respondents expressing intent to stay, only 2 percent indicated that they didn't trust their managers. Of the latter group, only 45 percent said that they trusted their managers completely, suggesting to us that even among this group, there remains a lot of unspent discretionary effort.[1]

As touched on in chapter 1, much has occurred over the last twenty years to erode trust in the workplace. Yet, all the while, the degree of trust required to permit Oomphing remains basically the same. A few hints follow.

TRUST BOOSTERS: THINGS THAT ADD TO THE "TRUST ACCOUNT"

1. Integrity. Nothing builds (or deflates) trust within and about an organization like the presence (or lack) of integrity . . . honesty, candor, character. This is something that can neither be faked nor pulled out for use only when it's convenient to do so. It is no more or less than doing what's right, even when no one is looking.

2. Shared goals and information. When goals are clearly understood and information is readily made available about progress toward those goals, cynicism and second-guessing are reduced considerably, even if one doesn't particularly agree with the goals. In like fashion, the very practice of listening to people validates them and strengthens their belief that they are being dealt with forthrightly.

3. Consistency. In order for us to really trust, what we see with our eyes and feel in our gut must coincide with what we've read or heard. The presence of any daylight between them is like a small crack on the leading edge of an aircraft wing, with the net result being analogous to what happened to the shuttle Columbia upon reentry into the earth's atmosphere.

According to Diane Raines, chief nursing officer of Baptist Health Systems, Jacksonville, Florida, "If it's a tight budget year, we might say that we'd like to send more people to outside seminars for training, but we have to put all our resources at the bedside. People will understand that and respect that, but only if we're clear in telling them what we're doing and why. If they see this going on, but they don't understand and respect it, their morale and motivation slump, and you're not going to see as much discretionary effort. If they do understand, they'll continue to go above and beyond. The best way to punch a hole in this would be to tell them this, and then see all the senior executives go off on a boondoggle somewhere. We're careful not to let that kind of thing happen."

4. Example. The ability to earn the trust of others in an organization depends heavily on the kind of example being set by the organization's leaders. In a 1997 survey conducted by DDI of fifty-seven client organizations, of the four groups rated (peers, leaders, other teams, and senior management), senior management was the least-trusted group (with an average score of 4.51 on a 7-point scale).[2]

5. Discipline. Trustful organizations, regardless of size, simply do not tolerate those who lack integrity. In 1978, having just accepted a job with FedEx, I was summoned to Memphis by my new boss, a blunt-talking former FBI agent by the name of Harry Keenan. The whole purpose for our very brief meeting was for him to look me in the eye and communicate the following message: "We've got a lot to get done in the months and years ahead, and I need your help to do that. As we begin to work together, it is important for me to know that you understand something clearly. I expect you to make mistakes. But you must understand that there are two kinds of mistakes. The first is the kind you make up here (pointing to his head). I expect you to make lots of these, because if you don't, you're likely not going fast enough or being bold enough. The other kind is the ones you make down here (pointing to his heart). Please understand that the first one of those will be your last." Assuring him that the message was loud and clear, I headed back to New York and began a very challenging and rewarding eleven-year experience.

Trustful organizations also have the discipline to prepare relentlessly. World-class mountaineer Michael O'Donnell relayed a story about one of his climbs with his friend and climbing partner Erik Weihenmayer. "In 2004, we were in Cortina, Italy, doing a very difficult 2,200-foot dead-vertical climb. At one point, when we were well up the face and I was belaying Erik, all of a sudden I was struck by the fact that I'm up here in the middle of nowhere, all alone, with a blind guy. He's got my life in his hands, and his is in mine."

O'Donnell then added that the realization left his mind as quickly as it had entered, owing chiefly to their mutual trust. When asked how that trust was built and nurtured, he talked at length about their preparation. "He (Erik) prepares meticulously, and when you see that, you know he's genuine, and he's committed . . . and he knows I do the same. We do not go into these situations half-a**ed. We pay attention to all the little sh*t. We're fully committed to the process, and one another—100 percent committed."

6. Forgiveness. During the time we spent with Chick-fil-A president and COO Dan Cathy, we asked him lots of questions about what, in his opinion, leads people to lend that precious increment of discretionary effort to his family's business, in pursuit of Chick-fil-A's mission. We talked a lot about purpose and mission, about intrinsic motivation, and, of course, about honor, dignity, and respect.

One night, while flying eastward across Arkansas, Dan uttered the word "forgiveness." Hoping he wasn't suggesting that he had committed some error as the pilot that would require forgiveness, I asked him to expound. As soon as we landed, he did.

> OK, I've been thinking a lot about this discretionary effort thing we've been talking about all week. And here's what I think.

People are all different. You have to motivate people differently. You know that. What causes one person to expend discretionary effort may not have the same effect on someone else. What we have to do is hire the right people, and then create the environment that does the best job of capitalizing on their internal triggers of motivation.

For some people, forgiveness is a motivation. Once you've been forgiven of something, especially if it's pretty serious, you can't help but remember that. And sometimes that will cause you to go above and beyond for the person who gave you that second chance.

He then reached back into his memory, to when he was a young man, and he and his father were walking around the original Dwarf House restaurant (the forerunner of Chick-fil-A) one evening, inspecting the premises. It seems that a gaze upward revealed a fresh collection of empty beer cans on the roof of the Dwarf House. As alcohol never has been on the menu of the Dwarf House, or Chick-fil-A, it was determined that, unfortunately, the spent vessels most likely came from an employee engaging in off-label activities on the job.

Once you've been forgiven of something, especially if it's pretty serious, you can't help but remember that. And sometimes that will cause you to go above and beyond for the person who gave you that second chance.

As much as Truett didn't like to think of any of his beloved employees drinking at work, he suspected a middle-aged fellow named James. When Truett confronted him, he gently extracted a genuine confession.

What happened next owes to James's greatly improved judgment in having told the truth about the incident and to Truett's exceptional maturity. Name any employer. Drinking beer on the clock and then littering the premises with the evidence would pretty much be grounds for dismissal without intervention from even the most liberal of unfair labor treatment folks.

Instead, Truett forgave James. James didn't get a lecture about how wrong it was to drink on the job. Truett figured James was an adult and therefore knew what he did was wrong. He didn't get fired. He didn't get written up. He barely got a reprimand. He got forgiven. Which is not to say his deed got overlooked.

By forgiving rather than firing James, Truett took the bond of trust between the two men to a completely new level, something that was not lost on James over the balance of his long career with the company.

TRUST BUSTERS

1. Contradiction. Most folks we come in contact with in the workplace are mature, responsible adults who understand that life is not one giant tea party. They can appreciate the fact that organizations have their rules, norms, and expectations. What they do not appreciate is people who sing one tune and dance to another. Whether this condition relates to a systemic defect or insincerity, it does not inspire trust.

2. Management aloofness. It is difficult to respect, let alone trust, people who put themselves on a pedestal or remain out of the fray.

3. Selfishness. People who are always looking out for their own interests don't make especially good team players because of the trust deficit their behavior induces.

4. Misguided rewards. Too often, in our quest to provide a performance-based rewards system, we wind up creating a process that puts people who should be cooperating into a competitive mode. Though we are all for competition, it must be carefully directed. People who need to be in a trustful, cooperative relationship ought not be incrementally inspired to compete with one another. If the guy who is my "catcher" in a high-wire act is incented for personal style points rather than his reliability in catching me, we have a problem, don't we?

CHAPTER SUMMARY

1. Trust is the lubricant that frees people up to go all out (Oomph!) in pursuit of their very best work.
2. People will not expend discretionary effort for managers who practice or tolerate untrustworthiness.
3. Trust Boosters: Integrity, shared goals and information, consistency, example, discipline, and forgiveness.
4. Trust Busters: Contradiction, management aloofness, selfishness, and misguided rewards.

MONDAY MORNING, 8am

Pour a fresh cup of coffee, and ponder the following questions:

1. What steps have you taken to clearly demonstrate that trust is a vital part of how you want to run your organization? How do you demonstrate to the outside world that you are trustworthy? How do you demonstrate to employees that you trust them?

2. Where might a "trust deficit" be slowing you or your people down?

3. How might you use trust to a competitive advantage?

11

CARING

The biggest thing that makes my staff work hard for me—and this is the God's honest truth—is that I care about these people. Even the ones who tick me off. I still care about them. I still want them to be OK and to do well. They know that, and they'll always work hard for me. And they know that I'll work hard for them. —Nick Mendez, fitness manager, 24 Hour Fitness

THIS EFFORT'S FOR *YOU*

Contrary to what you may think, this is not the touchy-feely chapter. In our view, there's nothing touchy-feely about caring. It's not fake, faddish, soft, or weak. It can be hard to do and, for some of us, even harder to show.

No. There's nothing touchy-feely about caring. But we know that workers reserve their best effort for someone they know *cares* about them as a person.

When we grilled focus groups on the personal attributes that, in their views, accounted most for Oomph!, one of the attributes that got the most votes was caring. A machine operator in a manufacturing plant put it best, "All I need to know is that you give a sh*t about me, as a person. If you do, you've got me. I'll do whatever it takes."

"All I need to know is that you give a sh*t about me, as a person. If you do, you've got me. I'll do whatever it takes."

People can be very forgiving. They'll overlook stupidity, confusion, cluelessness, poor judgment, harsh words, and even bad food in the employee dining room. But they will not overlook an uncaring manager. At the end of the day, caring is the final arbiter as to whether or not Oomph! is going to be expended.

Don't confuse caring with coddling. It's not pampering. And it's not something we do in an effort to win a popularity contest. But caring involves an element of compassion—the awareness of the suffering of another, coupled with the wish to relieve it.[1] It doesn't matter whether that compassion comes from a sense of altruism, pragmatism, or both. It's pretty clear that leaders who have compassion for those they lead, and manifest that compassion through kind words, actions, and other considerations, get more Oomph! than their colder, less caring colleagues.

Undemonstrated care is kind of like chocolate still in the wrapper—it's great stuff, but it doesn't do anybody any good.

Interviewer to jazz legend B. B. King: *You know, B. B., your music isn't for everybody. Not everybody likes you.*
B. B. King: *I'm not sure anybody likes me, but my mama. And she may be jivin'.*[2]

Caring can't be faked. Though we know it gives rise to discretionary effort, we doubt that you can turn it on purely for that purpose. We're reasonably sure that caring can't be taught. You either care or you don't. But if you do care, and you're not sure how to show it (undemonstrated care is kind of like chocolate still in the wrapper—it's great stuff, but it doesn't do anybody any good), here are some things that might help.

LEADERS WHO CARE TELL THE TRUTH, EVEN WHEN IT HURTS

Of all the myriad images that flood the minds of most Americans and others from the horrific events of September 11, 2001, one stands out for us in its ability to make the connection between caring and telling the truth.

As the day drew to a welcome close, under the glare of floodlights illuminating the ruins of the World Trade Center towers, a reporter asked then-New York mayor Rudy Giuliani, "Do you have any estimate, sir, of how many casualties there will be?"

Spurning the usual "official-speak" often associated with the public comments of elected officials, Giuliani responded simply, straightforwardly, and with compassion, "The number of casualties will be more than any of us can bear."

He told the truth. The pure, ugly, unadulterated truth. It hurt, yet it had to be told.

Regardless of what you think of Giuliani's political persuasions (or aspirations), how he manages his personal life, or anything else about the man, there seems to be universal agreement that on 9/11, the mayor of New York City cared. He told the truth; he was out there, visible, intimately involved, taking action, listening, and—above all—communicating with a frightened city and nation. He told us what he knew, what he didn't know, and when he'd get back to us with more information.

BLOWING THE TRUTH—CONSOLIDATED FREIGHTWAYS

Telling the truth does not, in and of itself, constitute caring.

In our first book, *Contented Cows Give Better Milk*, we selected Consolidated Freightways as one of our "Common Cow companies"—organizations that have done little if anything to distinguish themselves as employers of choice. Little did we know that a few short years later, CF's financial and other failures would cause it to file for bankruptcy and shut down all its U.S. operations.

On Friday, August 30, 2002, all thirteen thousand U.S. employees of Consolidated were instructed to call a toll-free phone number the following Monday—Labor Day—to receive an important message. Following is a partial transcript of that recorded message:

> Hello. This is John Brinko. I'm speaking to you today from CF corporate headquarters in Vancouver, Washington. Today is Monday, September 2, 2002.
>
> Thank you for dialing in on this holiday weekend. I hope you and your family are enjoying your time together. I have some extremely urgent and sad news to share with you today. A decision has been reached to discontinue all CF's U.S. operations. Immediately. Since we no longer have the financial resources to pay employees and continue operations, please do not report to your terminals tomorrow. All U.S. terminals will not be open tomorrow morning, and you should not report, since your employment ends immediately.

I'm sorry for this action, but we have no other choice, due to a lack of financial resources.

Mr. Brinko really has a way with words, doesn't he? Our favorite part is "I hope you and your family are enjoying your time together." He should have added, "Because there's going to be a lot more of it!"

Sure. You have to tell people the truth. But you *don't* have to do *that*. John Brinko may have thought it was his duty as CEO to drop the bombshell. It would have been better dropped by each station manager to his or her team, in the facility they would soon be vacating.

DOWN 'N DIRTY

When telling the truth, especially when the news is bad:
- Do it earlier rather than later.
- Don't e-mail it.
- Don't phone it in.
- Do it in person. It doesn't have to be in private, but it should be in person.

IF YOU CARE, YOU'RE THERE—"SITTING ON A FOOTLOCKER"

One of the legendary leaders from whom we've drawn immeasurable inspiration over the last number of years is the late Melvin Zais, a general in the U.S. Army who served as commander of the 101st Airborne Division in Vietnam in 1968. After the war, and toward the close of his illustrious military career, Zais spent much of his time speaking in the military educational establishment on—of all things—the role of a caring leader.

In one particularly eloquent delivery before a group of officers assembled at the Armed Forces Staff College, Zais exhorted his audience to simply be out there, with their troops, especially when they were undertaking a particularly difficult or important job.

When you're getting ready for the annual inspection and you know these guys are GI-ing the barracks, and you know they're working like hell, and it's Sunday night. If you'll get out of your warm house and go down to the barracks, and wander in to see 'em work, and just sit on a footlocker. You don't have to tell 'em, "You're doin' a great job." Just sit on a footlocker and talk to one or two soldiers, and leave. They'll know that you know that they're workin' like hell to make you look good.[3]

SHOWING UP FAR FROM HOME

Regardless of your (or our) views on the War in Iraq or George W. Bush, it's a pretty sure bet that, were General Zais still alive, he would have been pleased to see the commander-in-chief of the U.S. military borrow a lesson from his playbook in November of 2003. Under cover of darkness and a few fibs about his holiday plans, the president, with a baseball cap pulled low over his face, sneaked past reporters, made a clandestine trip to Baghdad, and delivered some shock and awe of his own by joining about six hundred troops for Thanksgiving dinner.

We neither know, nor care, what motives may have prompted the trip. No one knows how much of a factor the visit will be in the ultimate outcome of the war (a war that continues to rage, as we write this, with no clear end in sight.) But we do know this: Within hours, if not minutes, of Air Force One's landing in Baghdad, every soldier in the theatre knew that the guy who sent them there had left his family and a warm house in Texas, flown halfway around the world, and landed in a still dangerous place to be with them on a holiday. The overwhelming majority of them seemed to appreciate that. As a result of that visit, we can be fairly certain that each of them gained assurance that they had not been forgotten, that their work matters, and that someone north of them in the food chain cared enough to show up.

Now, here's the question—and the lesson—for us all. How many of our own employees have enjoyed that same feeling in recent weeks, or even months? How many times have we gone out of our way to spend a few minutes with them, on their turf, acknowledging the contribution they make? How often have we made time to sit and listen about something that's important to them, or inquire about something that's bothering them? When was the last time they heard those two little words (thank you) that feel good to everyone's ears?

Whether your political views favor the donkeys or the elephants, there just might be a good reminder here for all of us. In our increasingly speed-conscious, wireless, uptight world, spending a few minutes sitting on that footlocker can be priceless. It benefits not just the folks we visit but—as evidenced by what appeared to be tears welling up in the president's eyes that Thanksgiving Day in 2003—the one doing the sitting as well. And we don't have to risk getting shot to do it, either.

SHOWING UP CLOSE TO HOME

Another guy who "gets" the visibility thing is Terry Andrus, CEO of East Alabama Medical Center, in the small town of Opelika. While the nursing profession in the U.S. has an annual average turnover rate greater than 50 percent, EAMC's typically runs less than one-fourth of that. Perhaps one contributor to the loyalty, quality, and Oomph! that comes from this hospital's workforce is what everyone there calls "T.A.'s Rounds."

Every day that Andrus is in town, without exception, he comes in early so that he can spend at least an hour of his day walking around, talking to people, mostly listening. That's enabled him to lead this hospital for more than twenty years while the institution has done remarkable things in terms of patient care and employee commitment.

Occasionally Andrus faces skepticism from onlookers who say, "How can you justify spending that much time just 'visiting' with folks, when you're the CEO? How do you get your job done?" Andrus's retort—and he really believes this—is "that *is* my job."

SPECIAL CARE WHEN TIMES ARE TOUGH

My seatmate on a flight from Atlanta to Albany, New York, was a young woman who seemed distraught and distracted. After spilling coffee all over both of us, she apologized profusely, introduced herself as Victoria, and then told me that she was on her way to Vermont to be with her fiancé, who was in a hospital there.

A cameraman on a film crew making a documentary on tourism in the Green Mountain State, her intended, a guy named Joe, had been with the production company for only a few weeks, and this was his first project with them. The morning before, he failed to report for breakfast at the hotel, and the film's director, Mel, and his other colleagues grew concerned. Neither phone calls nor knocks on his hotel room door produced any response, and when the hotel manager finally opened the door for Mel, they were shocked to find Joe sprawled on the floor in what was later determined to be a diabetic coma.

Mel called Victoria, bought her a ticket from Phoenix to Albany, met her at the airport, drove her to the hospital in Vermont, and put her up in the hotel where they were staying. Two days later, Joe was well enough to resume filming. Victoria stayed on to make sure he was as well as he thought he was, and at the end of the week, they all returned to Phoenix with twenty hours of film in the can.

There are few connections in the world of business clearer than the one between how an organization treats its employees and how those employees treat their customers.

I know the outcome of this story because Victoria, a realtor in Phoenix, gave me her business card, seemed to appreciate my concern, and actually e-mailed me the following week to let me know how things had turned out. I kept up with her and Joe for about a year after that, and still get an occasional e-mail from one or the other of them. They got married as scheduled, and Joe still shoots films for Mel.

Artists like Joe aren't known for tying themselves down to the same production company for long periods of time. In fact, Joe had shot for no fewer than nine separate companies in his twelve-year career as a cinematographer. But none like the company he had joined in Phoenix just weeks before collapsing in the Vermont hotel.

Joe told me, "I get offers all the time. That's how this business works. But after the way this company has treated me, I think long and hard every time something else comes along. I hope I don't need it again—what Mel did for us in Vermont—but if I do, I just don't think I'd get it anywhere else."

THE CARING-CUSTOMER CONNECTION

We want you to look for opportunities to help when a team member is having to endure a hardship. We want you to go above and beyond for that person. And when you do, you will have their full attention when you start talking about going above and beyond for our customers. —Dan Cathy, president and COO, Chick-fil-A, Inc., to a group of company managers

There are few connections in the world of business clearer than the one between how an organization treats its employees and how those employees treat their customers. Treat your employees with respect and you're likely to see them respecting your customers. Take care of your workers' needs and they'll probably do a better job of taking care of your customers' needs. Do more than is expected for a member of your team and, as Dan Cathy points out, that member is likely to do more than is expected for your customers—internal and external.

DOWN 'N DIRTY

If you care . . .
- You tell people the truth. Blowing smoke up somebody's nose isn't caring, it's cowardice.
- You don't expect others to pay for your mistakes.
- You don't allow anyone to abuse or humiliate your teammates.
- You listen, really listen.
- You show up (in person) when people are having a tough time.
- You go above and beyond for them, especially if you expect them to go above and beyond for your business.

EAST ALABAMA MEDICAL CENTER—CORNERSTONE SOCIETY

Some years ago, a woman employed at East Alabama Medical Center lost her home in a fire. Immediately, and spontaneously, her co-workers collected among themselves enough money—not to replace her loss—but to make it a lot easier for her to start to get her life back on track after this terrible ordeal. From that reflex of kindness emerged what is now called the Cornerstone Society, an employee-run foundation that exists to help employees in times of crisis.

Funded through voluntary payroll deductions (with a high participation rate), occasional fundraisers, and managed by one full-time professional, Cornerstone distributes about $125,000 per year to hospital employees who need it. Fires, storms, illness, accidents, and death of family members are all examples of qualifying events.

About the time of our most recent visit to EAMC, the society was helping an employee who had a ten-year-old child with terminal cancer. Through a special jewelry sale, Cornerstone provided income continuation for the employee so she could stay at home to provide end-of-life care for the child. Says EAMC's CEO Terry Andrus, "We think Cornerstone sends a powerful message to all of our people that says, 'If, for whatever reason, something happens that's beyond your control, we're there to help.'"

CARING MATTERS

Nick Mendez is a twenty-five-year-old manager with 24 Hour Fitness, a large national chain of health clubs headquartered in Dallas. A veteran of the wars in both Afghanistan and Iraq, this former member of the Army's elite Ranger unit began working as a personal trainer for the company shortly after returning from his final deployment. In just under a year, Nick rose through the ranks to become fitness manager at one of the chain's locations. In recognition of his emerging leadership, he was chosen to represent 24 Hour Fitness as a torch runner for the 2006 Winter Olympics in Torino, Italy.

"I loved my men to death," he told us. "The decision to leave the Army was a hard one for me to make, but it was time for me to come back." Nick's first experience as a formal leader, in the Army, taught him about the burden good leaders bear for the well-being of those who follow them.

"I always thought about them as part of my family," he told us. "They're not just a bunch of soldiers. They're husbands, fathers, brothers, sons, boyfriends to *somebody.* I felt an incredible responsibility. As a leader in the Army, you want to do everything you can to make sure they can come back home to their families, in good condition, with all the body parts they went over there with. It was a big deal for me. I knew that how these guys were led made some of the difference as to whether or not they came back home."

Without missing a beat, Nick brought his "caring skills" back to the trainers who report to him now at 24 Hour Fitness. "One of my trainers got hit one week with a triple whammy. Two of his clients suddenly moved away, and another one had to quit working out during chemotherapy for cancer. None of this was the trainer's fault, or under his control. But he still lost a lot of business, and that cut into his paycheck."

Nick knew the trainer was a good enough salesman to replace the lost business within a month or two, but he wanted to help speed up the restoration process. Nick got out there and started walking the floor at the club, talking this guy up to clients who weren't using a personal trainer, telling them what a great trainer he is, what a great guy he is. He was able to build his business back in about two weeks.

"I didn't say anything to him about it. He knew what was going on. Right after that, I started noticing he was pitching in a lot more, cleaning up, helping others, doing things he really didn't have to do."

Oomph! on.

CHAPTER SUMMARY

1. At the end of the day, caring is the final arbiter that determines whether or not discretionary effort is going to be expended.
2. Caring is not coddling.
3. If you care, you:
    a. Tell people the truth.
    b. Don't expect others to pay for your mistakes.
    c. Don't let anybody abuse or humiliate your teammates.
    d. Show up (in person) when people are having a tough time.

MONDAY MORNING, 8am

1. Ask yourself, "Do I care—do I really care? How do I know I care? How do *others* know I care?"

2. Consider the question: "As an organization, how do we demonstrate to our employees and our customers that we care?"

3. Now, identify one action step you are willing to take to strengthen your performance with regard to each of the above questions.

SECTION FOUR

OOMPH! LEADERSHIP

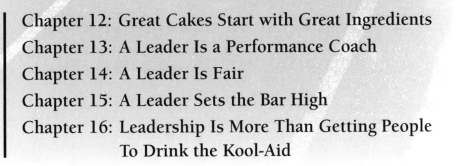

12

GREAT CAKES START WITH GREAT INGREDIENTS

Where you have motivated officers and soldiers, you have an army punching above its weight. Where you don't have motivated officers and soldiers, you have an army punching a clock. —Thomas L. Friedman, columnist, *New York Times*[1]

Most organizations proudly claim that "people are our most important asset." When one considers the alternative (admitting that our people are, well, pretty average), continued use of this tired but well-intentioned expression seems ensured. Truth be known, people aren't our business's most important asset—far from it. The *right* people might be, but not people in general.

This is a lesson that's not been lost on the world's very best-performing organizations. After a decade of examining the management and leadership habits of many of these businesses, we can offer one "iron law" they all adhere to—they are absolute zealots about recruiting and hiring the right people for their organization. Great cakes start with great ingredients.

Arguably, *the* most important decision any manager makes is determining who does—and who does not—get hired. Following are a few things they do to ensure that this decision turns out well. And before you ask, these things are indeed applicable, whether your business has two employees or 200,000.

HIRE FOR FIT

We've all heard about the "war for talent." Looking out at the labor force demographics for the next decade or so, most of us could benefit from a not-so-gentle reminder that people are still free to choose their place of employment, and that the war for talent is alive and well.

Smart leaders search far and wide for people who practically ooze talent, because it's important. But they know there's something even more important—finding those folks who, by virtue of pace, preference, values, chemistry, and the like, actually "fit" their particular organization. They realize that, because of culture and chemistry,

"Passion beats pedigree."

most—repeat, most—people will not be happy, productive, or successful working at their place. They also know that, in the majority of cases where the hiring decision doesn't work out, the cause has more to do with chemistry than talent. In the words of that great management scholar, Jon Bon Jovi, "Passion beats pedigree."

Southwest Airlines has absolutely beat its competitors' brains out for three decades with this one, by hiring people who—get this—make it their habit to listen, smile, care, and say thank you. Yes, they worry about talent, and thank goodness make it a point to hire people well-skilled in the craft of flying and fixing airplanes. Unlike many of their competitors, though, Southwest believes it's fundamentally stupid to lock cranky, ill-mannered employees into a steel tube with paying customers for hours on end. For that reason, applicants—including those with a jillion hours of pilot-in-command experience—who fall even a wee bit short on the four aforementioned characteristics aren't going to work for Southwest, period.

BEWARE THE WRONG FILTERS

Just as damaging as letting people in who don't fit is the practice of keeping people out simply because they don't conform to some irrelevant filter unwittingly (or in some cases, quite wittingly) imposed on the selection process. Insisting, for example, on "an aggressive spirit" for a job in which aggression has never been demonstrated to predict success has the potential to screen out highly qualified candidates who just happen to possess a calmer nature.

Imagine the outcome if, in 2006, the judges of *American Idol* had arbitrarily decided that no gray-haired singers would win that year's competition. Setting aside your own opinion of Taylor Hicks's talent, you'd have to acknowledge that the results would have been different.

Focusing on traits and qualities that don't matter while ignoring real qualifications is like judging a wine by the number of syllables in its name. Under such a plan, alas, the poor Gewurtzraminer would never have had a chance.

When we screen out talent because, for example, the candidate didn't graduate from a school on our "A" list (or maybe didn't graduate at all); doesn't have the right "look"; or is suspected of harboring political views to the left or right of our own (in a job that has nothing to do with politics), we may be denying ourselves, and our organizations, someone who does, in fact, fit, in every way that matters. In so doing, we lose talent to the competition.

FORGET ABOUT THE LIMP[2]

Gen. Nathaniel Greene was the youngest general in the American army during the Revolutionary War. He was an extremely intelligent, multitalented, and highly self-educated man. A childhood accident had left him with a stiff right leg and a very noticeable limp. The limp didn't bother him, but it seemed to bother everybody else.

He was highly committed to the cause of American independence from Great Britain, and he was determined to become an excellent fighter, although he had no previous war experience. He read voraciously, studying everything he could get his hands on to learn military tactics and the art of war. He took a leading part in organizing a unit of the Rhode Island militia, only to be told that his bad leg disqualified him from being an officer in the very militia he had helped to found. Although he was profoundly disappointed, he accepted their decision and resolved that if unacceptable as an officer, he would willingly serve in the ranks. Shouldering an English musket he had bought in Boston from a British deserter, he marched as a private in company drills for eight months until it became obvious to everyone in the unit that for a man of such knowledge, ability, and talent, *it would be best to forget about the limp.*

> *Southwest believes it's fundamentally stupid to lock cranky, ill-mannered employees into a steel tube with paying customers for hours on end.*

117

Almost overnight, he was given full command of the Rhode Island regiments, which were highly instrumental in winning the War of Independence.

NEVER (EVER!) STOP RECRUITING

Highly successful leaders do a relatively short list of things very well, and they do them consistently. One of those things is recruiting. They realize that if they wait until a big new contract lands or someone leaves to begin the recruiting process, they are hugely disadvantaged. Within five minutes of finding yourself short-staffed, your judgment begins to erode and, instead of waging a war for talent, your primary concern has to do with "putting butts in seats."

In many respects, recruiting is a lot like sport fishing, to which I am seriously addicted. Because I have yet to have a fish voluntarily jump into the boat, unaided by tackle or effort on my part, I've learned to keep casting and keep my lure in the water. If a particular lure isn't working, I change it, change the method of retrieve or the depth in the water column, or move the boat, but in any event, I keep fishing!

In a recent speech to a group of restaurant operators, I encouraged them to recruit at the same frequency at which they put out the trash and count the cash. That advice would serve the rest of us just as well. Sadly, I was reminded of this recently when I stopped for breakfast around 8 AM

> *Within five minutes of finding yourself short-staffed, your judgment begins to erode and, instead of waging a war for talent, your primary concern has to do with "putting butts in seats."*

at the Chili's Restaurant in terminal A at Atlanta's Hartsfield Jackson airport and was informed, "We are on a forty-minute wait (for breakfast!) because we only have three servers on duty."

One of the most common, dysfunctional, and easily remedied violations of the "Never Stop Recruiting" rule is the utterly nonsensical practice of periodically refusing to accept applications. On more than one occasion, we've turned up at a corporate location only to find a sign posted on the front door of the establishment declaring, "We Are Not Currently Accepting Applications."

Of *course* you're accepting applications! To do otherwise assumes ALL of the following:

- We have the perfect workforce now. There is no possibility that we could improve the gene pool in any way by the addition of any other person currently living on planet Earth.
- All of our employees are 100 percent loyal, immortal, immune from injury and disease, and unaffected by family or other relationships that might necessitate their relocation to another part of the world.
- We do not anticipate any growth in our business and therefore can't imagine needing to augment our talent pool.

The odds of your company having an opening for a particular job at the precise moment that the perfect person happens to have an opening in his or her career are astronomical!

Refusing to even receive information about a potential addition to the workforce indicates a laziness and shortsightedness that no business can afford today. Imagine a charitable organization issuing the follow communication: "We are not currently accepting cash contributions. We have all the money we need right now, thank you. Check back with us later."

Companies that take this rule seriously have been known to hire an exceptional person, *even when they didn't have a specific need or position.* You read that right. We are not suggesting you put unnecessary people on the payroll and then give them busywork until you find something productive for them to do. But we *are* suggesting that you can make the best use of available talent by capturing that person on *his or her* schedule, not necessarily on your schedule.

Think about it: The odds of your company having an opening for a particular job at the precise moment that the perfect person happens to have an opening in his or her career are astronomical! Lest we burst anyone's bubble, if you're totally honest with yourself, *your* greatest qualification for the job you currently hold *may* be impeccable timing. Most organizations are staffed by chance. Exceptional ones use a more intelligent, forward-thinking process.

AN INTELLIGENT PROCESS

Several things happen when you begin recruiting on a constant basis, most of them good. For one, you adopt better methods and procedures. When you're not desperate—behind the power curve—you can pay the necessary attention to each aspect of the process, notably sourcing, screening, and interviewing.

Sourcing. Owing to the prevalence of smaller-sized businesses these days, most of us are able to avoid the mass hiring scenarios that are every recruiter's nightmare and focus instead on finding great people—the right people—one at a time. Sensible sourcing methods should include soliciting candidate referrals from existing employees, customers, and suppliers. In fact, if you've been diligent over time in using this network and rewarding—really rewarding—folks for referrals, you may never have to venture down the paid advertising path.

Screening. The screening process for most positions involves screening for tangible as well as intangible factors. If, in the case of a retail position, for example, some prior retail experience is required, does the person's job application or résumé indicate that they have it? Ditto for a requirement to be knowledgeable about particular lines of goods. If the person will be required to conduct business for you over the phone, arrange to do a phone-screening interview with the candidate before seeing him or her in person. If the candidate doesn't come across the right way with you on the phone, it will never work with a customer. To ensure a more valid (and defensible) process, work from a legitimate list of "must have" and "want" characteristics for each position, and scrupulously rate each candidate via this matrix. Trust us on this one—just do it.

Interviewing. Most of us wind up with sub-par interview results for one of two reasons: 1) we're not as prepared as we should be, and 2) we talk more than we listen. Actually, the two are related. Because we're ill-prepared, we spend precious time rambling, rather than getting to know the candidate.

Early in my career, as the result of a headhunter contact, I was invited to interview for a mid-level management position with Digital Equipment Corporation. As the position represented a fairly significant increase in responsibility and income versus my then-current job, I accepted the interview and went about the process of doing my own due diligence prior to showing up. Having flown from northern New Jersey, where I was living, to Boston's Logan Airport, I was picked up by one of Digital's helicopters and whisked to the front lawn of the company's offices in what used to be an old woolen mill in Maynard, Massachusetts. I was duly impressed.

After being ushered to the offices of the VP of HR (the guy for whom I would be working) for my interview, I waited, and waited, and waited, for an hour and forty minutes, with precious little explanation or apology. Bearing in mind the helicopter experience, I managed to choke back the slow burn I was doing inside.

When I was finally in this guy's office, he took a long, first-time-ever glance at my résumé, looked up, and said, "I see you went to South Charleston High School." "Yes," I replied, expecting to hear something about how he, too, had gone there, dated one of my classmates, or perhaps had attended a neighboring school. No such luck. Next came, "What did you study in college?" After the third such utterly stupid question by a wholly unprepared interviewer, I interrupted the guy and, in as polite a manner as I could muster, confirmed that he really would be the person I'd be reporting to if this interview went well. He was. "I don't quite know how to say this, and you've been nice to invite me here, but this isn't going to work. If your helicopter is still here, I'd like to get a ride back to Logan. If not, would you be kind enough to call me a cab?" I'd like to believe that even if I didn't already have a good job, I would have had the courage to do the same thing.

> *There is no reason for any individual to have a computer in their home.* —Ken Olson, CEO, Digital Equipment Corporation[3]

A good deal of time should go into planning the interview discussion. Based on a thorough review of the candidate's application form or résumé, construct a base list of questions from which to work. Some questions should

be behaviorally anchored to elicit responses that describe specific things the candidate has done; for example: "Tell me about a time when you handled an unreasonable customer," "Tell me about your most/least favorite jobs in the past," or "From start to finish, please walk me through your last unsuccessful sales call." Others can be broader in scope and more open-ended; for example: "Tell me what you expect to be doing in three years."

Treat every candidate as you would a guest in your home.

Perhaps the best advice we can offer is to treat every candidate as you would a guest in your home. Have all the necessary preparations made in advance so that when the guest arrives, you can spend quality time together, uninterrupted. Be realistic about the length of the interview appointment and your scheduling of contiguous activities. Unlike the guy at now-defunct Digital, bear in mind that one of the most inconsiderate things you can do to another human being is to waste his or her time. Aside from the obvious reasons for behaving this way, we would do well to remember that every interviewee represents a window (with a mouth) into the organization. Moreover, they are also a potential customer.

RE-RECRUITING

It seems axiomatic that one of the smartest things for managers to do is to remain in "recruiting mode" at all times. We pound this point in speeches and seminars and watch all the heads nodding in agreement, then stand by to hear the distant thuds as most of these well-intentioned folks fall off the wagon. It is not unlike all those New Year's resolutions to lose weight or stop smoking that are usually in serious jeopardy by the first of February.

In response, we'd like to offer some additional thoughts about recruiting, albeit from a bit of a different perspective. Clearly, one of the reasons we wind up behind the 8-ball in recruiting is that folks have the audacity to take their act elsewhere, and do it without a whole lot of notice. Though a few of these departures bring a sigh of relief, most do not. They can be realistically classified as "regrettable turnover." Some of the newly departed are on their way to markedly greener pastures, but most aren't. So why are they leaving? For one (or more) of the very same reasons people leave a marriage or other significant relationship . . . they are bored silly, or feel they've been abused, cheated, or taken for granted. Let's concentrate on the last one since it's probably the most prevalent.

The recruiting process has only begun when you've found the right person and convinced them to board your ship.

It has been suggested that a key strategy for maintaining a successful relationship is to continue the courtship long after the "knot has been tied." Assuming that there is some validity to this notion, most of us discontinue our recruiting at precisely the wrong time, before the game has even begun. That's right, we are suggesting—no, insisting—that the recruiting process has only *begun* when you've found the right person and convinced them to board your ship. Before the ink is even dry on all those forms from HR, another phase of recruiting—re-recruiting, if you will—should begin, if you are serious about getting this hard-won recruit off to a great start, turbo-charging their performance, and convincing them to stick around and stay productive for the long haul.

Following is a suggested regimen of re-recruiting measures designed to help you with this process:

Pre-start: Before the person's first day of employment, there are a lot of necessary as well as neat things you can get accomplished. (Remember the axiom about first impressions.) A few starters:

1. Within days of their acceptance of your offer, they should receive a welcome letter from the president of your company. You prepare it; the president will sign it. Trust us—you'll knock somebody's socks off. (Time required: Twenty minutes)

2. Whether it is via the Web or old-fashioned mode, get the HR recordkeeping taken care of before the person reports for work. The absolute last thing you want to do is ruin someone's first day on a new job with a bunch of administrative crap. When it comes to benefits enrollment, here's where high tech should be augmented by some high touch. Ask that someone involved with your organization's benefits administration speak with the person to ensure that they understand their benefits options, claims procedures, and the like. When they are through, test them on this knowledge to be sure they really understand it. (Twenty minutes)

3. If relocation is involved in the job change, arrange to have some groceries and basic supplies delivered to the person's new residence coincident with the move-in date. More than twenty years ago, I showed up at a new employee's home shortly after the moving van had departed. My purpose was merely to see if they needed anything. It turns out they did. With a toddler and a newborn, they were already running about two quarts low—on milk. I scared up some milk, bread, and a few other essentials, delivered them, and left. To this day, they mention the "milk thing" whenever we talk! (Thirty minutes/$100)

   Last year, my daughter and her family were treated in similar fashion by Master Chief Beckwith, who is in charge of Air Station Savannah. Shortly after her husband's joining the Coast Guard, and their arrival at their new duty station in Savannah, Georgia, Master Chief Beckwith personally delivered a huge basket of food, and toys for their infant daughter, in an effort to make his new recruit (and family) feel more welcome. Mission accomplished.

4. See to it that their work area is set up and squared away. Whether it's ID cards, keys, an e-mail address, computer passwords, tools, business cards, or what, this stuff can and should be taken care of before the person arrives for work.

5. Once someone has accepted a job, make sure they start receiving selected pieces of intra-company communication. If your company has an employee handbook, by all means send them a copy, and ask them to read it. See to it that they are enrolled in any required or recommended training, and advised as to the date(s). Invite them to come in at their convenience for a tour and to meet new co-workers. Encourage them to bring family members if they wish.

Day 1: With the traditional orientation stuff taken care of already, this day should be about making sure the new person understands—really understands—the relevance of their work, and letting them get started with it. Towards the end of the day, spend a few minutes with them to answer any questions they may have, and learn the name of anyone who has been particularly helpful to them on that day, so you can thank them appropriately. (Fifteen minutes)

Week 1: Ask a different person to take the new staff member to lunch each day during this week. ($150)

End of Week 1: Ask your boss to spend a few minutes with the new person in order to 1) reinforce their decision to come to work for Acme Widget and 2) offer support. (Twenty minutes)

End of Week 2: Spend some time with them in their work area to find out 1) what they have learned and 2) what help they need. (Sixty minutes)

End of Month 1: Ask your HR rep to take the new person to breakfast or lunch and discuss if they are finding the new job and work environment as they had expected it to be. If you don't have an HR professional, turn to someone else you trust. ($40)

Day 45: Review with the new person the performance expectations for their position, and ask for their candid self-assessment regarding their performance. Coach as necessary. (Forty minutes)

Day 60: Spend an hour working with the new person, or reviewing their work output. Coach as appropriate. (Sixty minutes)

Day 90 (and every ninety days thereafter): On a rotating basis, conduct coaching sessions in which you are addressing topics either defined by the employee or by you. (Sixty minutes)

Routinely: In addition to varied social interaction with your employees, we heartily recommend that you take time to acknowledge the special events in their lives, and in the lives of their family members and significant others. Those cards, notes, and phone calls take but a minute, and are SO significant to the recipient.

Oh, and another thing: Don't think you have the ten hours and $300 to invest in the first year of re-recruiting your new folks? Better brush up on your résumé-screening and interviewing skills.

CHAPTER SUMMARY

1. The choice of who does and does not wind up on the payroll is every manager's most important decision.
2. As Southwest Airlines has proven for better than thirty years, talent is important, but hiring people who fit your organization is critical.
3. You should always be in recruiting mode, as your options (and decisions) will be much better when someone decides to take their act elsewhere.
4. Work hard at maintaining good relations with your applicant sources.
5. When interviewing, don't forget why you were issued two ears and only one mouth!
6. A good tactic for keeping your new people productive and happy is to continue recruiting (actually, re-recruiting) them even after they've signed on.

MONDAY MORNING, 8AM

1. Check your calendar for the week. Do you have any interviews scheduled? If so, take twenty minutes (that's right) and plan the interview. If you don't have any interviews scheduled, get busy!

2. Answer the following questions:

    a. Have you determined what traits, qualities, and characteristics are essential to being successful and happy at your business?

    b. What measures are you taking to be sure—really sure—that everyone you hire fits your organization?

Corporate culture should never be an afterthought. It is the key driver of value creation. —Carlos Ghosn, CEO, Nissan Motors[4]

13

A LEADER IS A PERFORMANCE COACH

A leader has two important characteristics; first, he is going
somewhere; second, he is able to persuade other people to
go with him. —Maximilien François Robespierre

You're four minutes into the second half of the championship basketball game. The clock works, but due to a computer glitch, the digits representing the score are meaningless. The numbers are there, but they bear no resemblance to the actual score. You have an idea the game's close, but you don't know for sure. Worst of all, you don't know if you're winning or losing.

That's how it feels when an employee receives inaccurate performance feedback, or none at all. It certainly doesn't improve performance, and in today's more personally oriented workplace, people simply won't put up with managers who can't or won't master this aspect of their jobs. As Jan Carlzon, former president of SAS, the Scandinavian Airline, once put it, "An individual without information cannot take responsibility. An individual who is given information cannot help but take responsibility."

To give people a fighting chance of succeeding, we've got to offer credible, meaningful, bone-honest information about their performance in a timely and constructive manner. One of the most uncaring things we can do is *not* to tell someone they're doing a lousy job (or worse, tell them they're doing fine) and then, six months later, terminate them for doing a lousy job. If you do that, *you're* doing a lousy job.

And if they're doing a *great* job, for Pete's sake, take advantage of the added motivation they'll feel when they realize you've recognized it. Tell them they're doing a great job, exactly what they do that makes it a great job, and what other good things have happened because of it.

Your employees need and deserve regular, frequent, and informal feedback, as well as those infamous meetings to go over their written performance appraisals. An honestly brokered survey would likely reveal that most of us hate the amount of effort that is required in order to do these things right. Not unlike the sign in every dentist's office—"You don't have to brush and floss all your teeth, just the ones you want to keep"—we just need to get over it and do it. It's our *job*. Appraisal is a process, not an event. To make that process easier and more effective, remember that performance appraisals are more than filling out the form.

Performance appraisals are more than filling out the form.

Organizations that do an exceptional job of giving performance feedback see the process as a cycle. New employees should have an evaluation at the end of no more than ninety days. If both you and the employee decide at that point that the employment relationship is worth continuing on a more permanent basis, set up a regular cycle of performance monitoring, coaching, and evaluation.

One of the most grievous errors managers unwittingly commit is failing to give regular performance feedback. Though annual review cycles are pretty standard, six months is probably better, as that time frame offers the potential for earlier recognition of improved performance. Whatever you settle on, stick to it. Committing to a review date and then missing it sends an unmistakable signal that the person and his or her performance aren't all that important to you. Yikes!

Start the cycle by sitting down with your team member in a controlled environment, free from distractions and interruptions. Establish a set of mutually determined performance objectives that the employee will commit to accomplishing over the course of the cycle. Those objectives should be:

- Measurable.
- Achievable, but challenging.
- Something the person can get excited about, not just be resigned to.

Next, outline with the employee precisely how he or she will accomplish these objectives. Do it in real terms. Vague strategies and targets yield weak commitment and weaker results. Ask the employee what resources are needed to hit the mark, then see to it that they are provided.

Once you and the employee have agreed on the objectives and the action plans, put it in writing. Not because you don't trust each other, but because you've already got enough loose stuff rolling around in your head.

Now the real work begins.

During the cycle, your job is to monitor—not micromanage, monitor—provide support, answer questions, and do those things you've committed to. Schedule two or three strategically placed coaching sessions at regular intervals within the cycle. Get out your calendar and a pen. If it's a six-month cycle, at the end of, say, two and four months, sit down and evaluate where you are. If my objective is to hike from New York to San Francisco in six months, and four months into the journey, I've only shuffled through Cleveland, somebody's got some work to do.

Don't limit your coaching to those scheduled sessions. Be flexible and available to hear from your employee at any point along the way, or to offer support and course corrections whenever they're needed. In giving feedback, follow these guidelines:

- Give clear and accurate descriptions of the performance you have observed. Keep emotions out of it, and emphasize objective findings.
- Help the worker understand the "why."
- Focus on things the individual can change or control.
- Balance praise with correction, but be clear in the message. Don't let it become garbled, worrying that you'll offend by stating the truth.

Never ask your players to play without a scoreboard.

A training classroom in a manufacturing plant where I once conducted a leadership seminar was adorned with a banner bearing these familiar words, "Knowledge is power." After we covered the issue of performance feedback, the training manager changed it to read, "Knowledge about my performance is the power to improve."

Give your people the power to improve with clear, accurate, and helpful feedback. Never ask your players to play without a scoreboard.

A DOSE OF REALITY

Through the first few years of the twenty-first century, television viewers have been witness to a rash of TV "reality" shows involving some form of competition in which a contestant is given some off-the-cuff performance assessment, then fired, branded "the weakest link," or summarily "voted off the island" at the conclusion of each episode.

OK. We know these shows are produced for entertainment value, but our hope is that we don't see a reverse migration from the screen to the workplace, as real-world viewer/managers seek to morph Acme Widget into a reality show.

Performance management and the occasional failure that results in the termination of someone's employment are anything but a laughing matter. Indeed, experience suggests that it's something managers struggle with more than just about anything else.

We get concerned about finding the right words with which to constructively criticize someone. Some worry about offending or risking their popularity. Others, known for having the properties of a heat-seeking missile, would do well to be a little more conscious of that. Some tread lightly because they fear a lawsuit, or claim they've been browbeaten by an overactive HR rep.

We blame our inability to conduct meaningful performance discussions on the inadequacies inherent in a fifty-cent form, or feel pressured to lower our own standards because of some easy-rating peers. Lacking control of our own emotions, some of us fly off the handle at the drop of a hat, demonstrating for everyone just what jerks we can be. We can always find a hundred other things more pressing than sitting down with someone and coaching them to better performance.

And what, you ask, does this have to do with Oomph!? A lot.

FORCED RANKING—IS IT A VIABLE PRACTICE?

Many organizations and managers continue to struggle with the notion of using "forced ranking" as a means of performance appraisal. For the uninitiated, this practice involves using a fixed rating structure whereby in any employee group, ten to twenty percent must be rated as either stars or slugs, and the remainder lumped into the "satisfactory middle." The practice has come about because over the years, managers have done a miserable job of being honest with people in reviews, classifying inordinately high numbers of people as stars, and almost no one as needing significant improvement in order to keep their job.

The problem is that forced ranking is just that—forced. It bears no more resemblance to reality than the cast of *The Office* bears to the people you work with. The entire premise on which it's based is utterly bankrupt—a nonexistent, irrelevant fantasy. It ignores the reality of people's individual performance, paying homage instead to the categories themselves.

Whether you opt for a forced ranking appraisal system or not, here are a couple of things to keep at the top of your mind. First, forget about changing the forms you use. Chances are they are just fine. For that matter, a blank sheet of paper (or no form at all) just might be the best place to start.

Second, one idea whose time has definitely *not* come is the so-called 360-degree review. On the surface it sounds like a winner for people to get their performance appraised by folks who work all around them. Unfortunately, whatever good might be accomplished is usually undone by the recipient's understandable musings about which of their co-workers decided to take a cheap—albeit anonymous—shot at them. There's also the difficulty in rationalizing the disparity between how one's peers and subordinates see them versus how their boss evaluates them. Wanna guess who weighs in more heavily, even though they may be outnumbered? And please, we don't need any other permutations (e.g., 180, 540, 720) of the 360-degree review, so let's just chop it off now before it grows into something really ugly.

Forced ranking is just that—forced.

Finally—forgive our being born in the 1950s—but even in the twenty-first century, performance reviews still ought to be a low-tech, high-touch affair. In other words, if you're going to do it, do it right. Sending somebody a review via e-mail is a long way from right.

VOTE 'EM OFF THE ISLAND

Even in an era of employment free agentry, when people are no longer wedded to their jobs, terminating, firing, canning, cutting, deselecting (choose your own favorite verb) someone is serious business. Our favorite euphemism is "releasing them back to the workforce." Many of the so-called experts would have us believe that the act of taking someone's work (and thus the source of their livelihood) away is a professional and thus impersonal act. Bullsh*t! Anyone who believes that has never been on either side of this equation. As but one case in point, we think it is a very safe bet that few people, if any, have EVER forgotten the name and face of the person who did it to them.

Two things are self-evident in this arena:

1. Everyone in a leadership capacity will some day find themselves telling someone that they "can't work here anymore," probably more than once, and

2. If doing so ever becomes easy, it's time to find a new line of work.

NOT EVERYBODY CAN PLAY ON YOUR TEAM

By definition, teams, departments, and companies are boundaried organizations characterized by certain standards, collective purpose, finite size, and membership requirements. No one has a lock on membership or an inherent right to be there. Most for-profit organizations strive to be a meritocracy where the status of one's rewards, privileges, and membership are driven by performance.

As such, these organizations, if they are to continue to exist within the bounds of their charter, must exclude or remove those who don't fit or whose performance or behavior fail to measure up. It falls to the leader to determine at what point the situation is irreconcilable. It's not something we particularly enjoy doing or look forward to, but it goes with the territory.

Painful as separating someone from the workforce is, opting not to carry it out when it is warranted brings far greater consequences.

Painful as separating someone from the workforce is, opting *not* to carry it out when it is warranted brings far greater consequences.

At the head of the list is the fact that this failure to act sends an unmistakable signal to the rest of the organization that the person's performance or behavior are OK, thereby diminishing the future standard for the entire group, and thus, its chances for survival. Similarly, it affirms for the team that they are no longer part of an elite organization. Convoluted as it may sound, it is also cruel to the individual who deserves to be removed, as in all likelihood, they already know that they don't fit or that the situation is not going to work. They just haven't figured out what to do about it yet, or perhaps are in denial.

WHEN YOU SEE A SNAKE, KILL IT

For six years, I had the absolute pleasure of working with one of the world's legendary leaders, Jim Barksdale of FedEx and Netscape fame. A native Mississippian, Jim is famous for his clear-cut, down-home style of communicating and a sizable list of folksy expressions we came to know as "Barksdaleisms." Though the origin of some of the expressions is uncertain, his skillful use of them nonetheless helped define the man for those of us fortunate enough to work with him.

One of those expressions, reputedly borrowed from Ross Perot is, "When you see a snake, kill it." Translation—when you see a threat, act. Don't draft a memo about snakes or commission a snake study. Kill the d*mned thing, now.

A derivative lesson for us in this case: When you realize that the situation is not going to work, act. Don't delay, as putting it off is committing a fraud against the individual and the organization.

BUT HOW?

In every case where I have found it necessary to remove a member of my staff, realization of the need to do so has been immediately accompanied by the same two feelings:

1. Dread for the day when I will have to carry out that decision, and
2. Guilt brought on by the realization that in some way I may have failed this person, and thus contributed to their demise.

For better or worse, my way of handling this situation has been to ask myself if a reasonable person would conclude that I have been fair and done what was practical and prudent to ensure this person's success. My mental checklist includes the following questions:

- Does the separation owe to chemistry (fit), behavior (conduct), or job performance?
- If it's "fit," am I basing my decision on legitimate factors, as opposed to personal preference or convenience?
- If it is a conduct issue, do I have a complete grasp of the facts and am I confident that others who are similarly situated get treated the same?
- Was the standard of conduct known?
- If performance-related, has the person been made aware of my expectations?
- Were those expectations reasonable?

- Have I taken and documented steps to make the employee aware that his or her performance was lacking, and how and in what timeframe it must improve?
- Has the individual been furnished the tools, training, time, and resources to succeed?

If the clear-eyed answer to each question is yes, I proceed.

Generally speaking, I've made it a practice to review both my decision and the letter of termination (always use one) with a competent HR professional before proceeding. They can keep you out of a lot of trouble. Notice, though that the operative term is "review," not "seek the approval of." Similarly, if the person's employment is governed by a contract, you will want to pay careful attention to its provisions.

Out of an abundance of respect for the fact that terminating someone's employment carries personal consequences, I do my best to be considerate of the individual. Though one cannot expect the person to ever feel that you've done them a favor by inducing a career change, I nonetheless want the person to feel that he or she has been treated with dignity, respect, and consideration.

If there is something the person needs on the way out the door that the company can in good conscience provide, I make an effort to do so. For example, even though there is no longer much stigma associated with being "fired," many people prefer to save face by resigning. Let them. Others may want or need some special consideration with regard to benefits, or the timing or wording of the announcement of their departure. Here again, if you can accommodate them without creating a huge expense or dangerous precedent, it seems wise to do so. What is not up for grabs is the fact that the relationship as we've known it is ending.

OUTPLACEMENT

For a very modest fee, you can secure the services of an outplacement counselor whose role is to provide career transition services—some handholding and objective insight during the early stage, help with the résumé and job search, a support network, and a place to go.

According to Lynn Jackson, VP of client services of Russell Montgomery Associates/OI Partners, "Utilizing an outplacement service can answer many of the questions about what to do and what not to do to successfully land a job. Outplacement is more than just teaching an employee how to find a job . . . it's learning the skills to manage a lifelong career."

THE MESSAGE

There is no nice way to tell someone that their employment with Acme Widget Co. has come to a screeching halt. Don't bother looking for one. There are some things that you can (and certainly should) do, however:

- Arrange for privacy.
- Anticipate as best you can the person's likely reaction and plan accordingly.
- If security is an issue, arrange for some professional help.
- Give thought to how (and when) the person will be allowed to collect personal belongings. Have some boxes handy.
- Have a minimalist (benign) announcement regarding the person's departure and interim arrangements prepared.
- Get your own thoughts and emotions very much in check.
- If you've opted to provide outplacement assistance, have the counselor nearby to begin providing assistance as soon as you have delivered your message.
- Keep your message short, to the point, and unemotional (see below).

> John, this is a conversation that I suspect neither of us wants to have, but we need to. After a good deal of thought, I have concluded that we need to make a change, and that change means that you will no longer be employed by Acme Widget Company.
>
> I am prepared to either accept your letter of resignation or give you a letter of termination today, whichever you prefer. Either way, the official date of your termination will be ___, but I am going to ask you to leave today. You will be paid through ___. Our benefits person (give them the person's business card) will be happy to address any questions you may have regarding benefit continuation. How would you like to proceed?

Don't debate or get drawn into the merits of the decision. Deliver the message and get off the stage.

BAD BOSSES ARE BAD BUSINESS

It is our hope that organizations everywhere will get serious about seeing to it that every soul placed into a leadership position has the tools, skills, character, and proclivity to lead others.

Over the years, we have consistently encouraged leaders to maintain the highest standards of conduct and performance for everyone on the payroll. Successful organizations don't suffer slackers, and they're careful not to put people in positions for which they're not suited. And that certainly includes managers who can't lead and inspire people to perform.

This might be a good time for a sober assessment of the process used at your place to identify, select, and train new leaders. Are you identifying people who have demonstrated both leadership and technical job skills, or just the latter? Are you identifying folks who *really* want to take on a leadership burden that can be difficult, lonely, and at times unpleasant, or those who merely want to make a little more money?

Does your selection process exclude those who, by virtue of character or reputation, simply cannot attract motivated followers in your organization? Does that process somehow capture and meaningfully use the opinions of the candidate's peers? If not, why?

Are you setting the kind of example you expect these people to follow?

Once selected, how are leaders prepared prior to assumption of their new duties? Please don't tell us you rely on the Donald Trump school of management development (i.e., lock everybody in the cafeteria, er, boardroom, initiate a food fight, and see who emerges). Seriously, are you devoting the time, attention, and resources to ensure that newly appointed leaders have a fighting chance of succeeding? What steps are you taking to provide them much-needed coaching during their initial weeks and months in the position? Are you setting reasonable goals and observing/evaluating performance in a timely manner? Perhaps most important, are you setting the kind of example you expect these people to follow?

If a bona fide non-leader has somehow been placed in a leadership position, and reasonable amounts of support and encouragement don't seem to be helping (quite often they won't, because things like courage, honesty, and humility can't be easily taught to adults), the individual should be "set free" and encouraged to pursue other opportunities more suited to his or her abilities. In other words, move them out. Do it humanely, but do it.

If this sounds harsh, or perhaps inconsistent with our premise, think again. There are few job conditions more miserable than working under the direction of an inept or uncaring leader. Moreover, the real purpose of all this is *not* to create a "happy happy" atmosphere but to generate better business outcomes through the efforts of a focused, fired up, capably led workforce.

Who among us would keep seeing a dentist who was lousy at administering anesthesia? Or would continue to employ a chef who, despite training and encouragement, never developed the ability to cook? So why, then, do so many of us tolerate people in management positions who have demonstrated a remarkable ineptness for managing people?

A strange and curious pattern has developed in many organizations whereby we:

1. Promote people who are good at what they do to positions of leadership, without regard for their ability to perform in a leadership capacity, or even their desire to do so.
2. Evaluate them primarily on their ability to episodically generate short-term results, and only secondarily, if at all, on their ability to lead people (which is ostensibly why that management position exists in the first place.)
3. If it becomes apparent that they have failed in their leadership roles, continue to tolerate them (even promote them) despite demonstrated incompetence in a fundamental function of the role.

Some of the most successful organizations on the planet know that being an effective people leader is a requirement—not a preference—of a manager's job. They've made these skills an absolute *condition of employment* for everyone in a management position, from first-line supervisor to CEO.

GE, under legendary leader Jack Welch, came down clearly on the side of leadership when it determined that those managers who failed to embrace the company's value of strong leadership skills would be required to change or leave.

Speaking of his own company's managers in *Fortune* magazine, Dell chairman Michael Dell said, "If you're a manager who is not addressing employee issues, you're not going to get promoted . . . or get compensation. And, if you consistently score in the bottom rungs of the surveys, we're going to look at you and say, 'Maybe this isn't the right job for you.'"[1]

We've all observed organizations that appear to turn a blind eye to struggling or misplaced leaders they have placed in positions of authority. Some of these managers are clueless, and deserving of pity. Others are abusive, insensitive, self-absorbed, pompous, callous, uncaring, weak-kneed, in over their heads, and not possessed of particularly good judgment. Some of them are just not very nice people. The high-falutin' technical term for a person who possesses three or more of the aforementioned attributes is "jerk," and let's face it, we've got some of them. And jerks just don't make good leaders. As one of our favorite leaders, Gen. Melvin Zais, put it, they are "a little person with a little job and a big head."

"If you're a manager who is not addressing employee issues, you're not going to get promoted . . . or get compensation."

One company we worked with had a senior manager, a person named Mark, who, despite formidable technical knowledge and skills, had managed to alienate just about everyone on his team over the course of the two years he'd been in his position. He was brilliant, but a lousy boss. Correction—he was a good boss, but a lousy leader.

The CEO, a fellow who regularly espoused strong leadership values, defended Mark's numbers and denied the negative impact he was having on the workforce. What started as an outward trickle of talent from his team soon developed into a hemorrhage. His employee survey scores were abysmal. The CEO did nothing, and poor morale ultimately caused a costly project failure. Still, Mark hung on for two more years, while the CEO kept hoping for improvement. When the inevitable separation happened, it was ugly, expensive, and several years too late.

Got managers in your outfit who are not fit to lead? Get them help, support, and training. Be bone-honest with them, and give them a reasonable amount of time to come up to speed. If they can't, or won't, do the right thing, before your best talent walks—to your most formidable competition.

TRAINING HELPS PEOPLE "NOT HOLD BACK"

On May 6, 2006, Officer Julie Welch of the Holly Springs, Georgia, police force, stopped a driver for failure of the driver and her passenger to wear their seatbelts. When the passenger got out of the car, it became apparent to

Officer Welch (and to the dashboard video camera trained on the scene) that this would be no ordinary traffic stop.

The behavior of the passenger—a man of six feet eleven inches—gave subtle clues to the officer—who stands five feet four inches—that he might have something to hide. Like a container of a mind-altering white powder he had stuffed into his pocket before he emerged from the vehicle.

While Officer Welch tried to fit the suspect with a pair of handcuffs, he wriggled away, knocking both of them to the ground. Then he got up and, unfortunately for him, ran into a nearby briar patch. He was barefooted.

A few weeks later, Officer Welch's story was featured on NBC's *Today Show*. The "hook," as the media would call it, was the "very tall man subdued by short woman" angle. The story might not have captured our attention except that anchor Ann Curry asked this question: "What made you *not hold back?*"

"We have an excellent training division," said Officer Welch, who handled the interview better than, say, the average media-coached U.S. senator subject to similar grilling. "Our training officer brings us the best training she can find."[2]

Thank you, Officer Welch, for helping us make a point. It's not just that people who are better trained know better how to do the job. That's a big duh. The point is that professionals who are *confident* in their *competence* are able to let forth with a boundless supply of energy, attention, and focus. Oomph!

Conversely, people who doubt their own ability to do a job particularly well can't help but—as Ann Curry put it—hold back. Ugh.

I also talked with Officer Welch, unconstrained by a producer of a morning news segment with a three-minute limit. She articulated some great lessons about the contribution of training to "not holding back."

"We're trained to recognize clues without consciously thinking about it," Officer Welch told me. Somewhere in her training, she had learned about something called the "no-look rule," which holds that if a person won't make eye contact with an officer in what would otherwise be a non-threatening situation (like walking down the street, or riding through a supermarket parking lot, as this suspect was doing), there might be something else going on. This behavior—looking for clues, and recognizing them—has become second nature for this officer, and others with similar training.

"Either that's from training," Welch said, "or the fact that I'm a mom." Either way, she's learned to look for something that gives rise to what law enforcers call an "articulable suspicion," something for which you can legitimately stop the person.

She stopped the car because its occupants weren't wearing seatbelts, a primary offense in the state of Georgia (meaning you can stop them for that and nothing else). But it's possible she might not have noticed had the passenger not so obviously turned away when he saw her patrol car. And she might not have asked the passenger to step out of the car had she not noticed his carotid artery throbbing heavily on the side of his neck—more evidence of something to hide.

"Our training also makes it easier for us to act with confidence, because we know what we can and cannot do with a suspect." She knew that she would be well within her rights to conduct a "Terry frisk" on the suspect (named, as she told us, for the 1963 Supreme Court case *Terry vs. Ohio*), in order to protect herself should the suspect be carrying a weapon. Had she not done the Terry frisk, she would have missed the three cocaine pipes in his pocket.

Julie Welch hadn't been *trained* to "not hold back"; her competence gave her the confidence to Oomph!

CHAPTER SUMMARY

1. Don't ask people to play without a scoreboard.
2. We all need and deserve regular, constructive, bone-honest feedback.
3. Performance objectives should be measurable, achievable (but challenging), and compelling.
4. Forced ranking is better in theory than in practice.
5. Not everyone can play on your team.
6. When you see a snake, kill it.
7. Bad bosses are bad business.
8. Training helps people not hold back.

MONDAY MORNING, 8AM

1. From now on, make leadership attributes and skills an absolute condition of employment for anyone in a management position at your place.

2. Begin an earnest look at how your organization conducts performance reviews. Are they timely, fair, honest, helpful?

14

A LEADER IS FAIR

*A foolish consistency is the hobgoblin of
little minds.* —Ralph Waldo Emerson

There are probably as many definitions of the concept of "fairness" as there are
models and variations of iPods (well, almost). In U.S. broadcast law, there's
an entire doctrine named for fairness. We hear people arguing that their
requests are nothing more than "fair and reasonable." Fox News Channel
describes its reporting as "fair and balanced,"
and satirist Al Franken used the same tagline
in the title of a book claiming that it's not. Fox
sued, saying that wasn't fair.

Children bellow "'sno fair!" in response to
any perceived injustice that comes their way
at home or on the playground. And the more
adult phrase "fair enough" is often retorted
when the one saying it really thinks "'sno fair,"
but wants to appear grown-up about it.

This is not a philosophy textbook and so
we're going to resist the temptation to rumi-
nate, on your dime, on the myriad meanings

> *If my default
> mode is Oomph!, but I see
> that you, as my manager,
> tolerate and even reward
> slackers and miscreants,
> my most likely response is
> to start powering back a
> notch or two.*

and implications of fairness in all its possible contexts. But we *will* take a stab
at defining "fairness" within the confines of leadership and the workplace,
and try to point out what fairness has to do with Oomph!

FIRST THINGS FIRST

The first topic that has to be broached in a discussion of fairness in the workplace is the grossly unfair practice of keeping non-performers on the payroll. This rampant practice undermines the ability of any leader to be seen as credible. It's unfair to poor performers, who would benefit from a dose of reality that might just put them on a better track, and to everyone around them, who has to pick up the slack . . . and the pieces.

Laws impact behavior, but not character. Fairness is an issue of character.

If my default mode is Oomph!, but I see that you, as my manager, tolerate and even reward slackers and miscreants, my most likely response is to start powering back a notch or two. Unless I am a person of most remarkable character, I can't help but reason that my extra effort isn't really necessary, and I'll divert some of that energy to other endeavors.

The remainder of this chapter assumes that you understand this first basic principle of fairness at work: Don't tolerate poor performers.

THE LAW—HARDLY A LOFTY STANDARD

I heard someone say on a radio broadcast once, in reference to a piece of impending legislation that "The law is hardly a lofty standard." Truer words were never spoken.

Legislatures and countless other rulemaking bodies have enacted a colossal mass of legislation designed to make employers behave in a fair manner with respect to their recruiting, hiring, employment, and separation practices. Not surprisingly, while these laws may have changed behavior to a degree, they've not, on the whole, succeeded in making employers act with any greater degree of fairness. Laws impact behavior, but not character. Fairness is an issue of character.

Good leaders understand the concept and benefits of fairness without any laws encouraging them in that direction. Good leaders don't discriminate unfairly. Not because there's a law prohibiting them from doing so, but because they think it's dumb.

CONSISTENCY DOES NOT EQUAL FAIRNESS

Early in my career as a human resources professional, I learned the mantra of all good HR people: Whatever you do, you must ensure that employees are treated fairly and consistently. The operative phrase was "fairly *and* (not or) consistently." It's a mindset that stuck with me for a long time, and I really never thought about it very hard.

Oh, there were those occasional episodes when doing the fair thing seemed about to collide with consistency (or common sense), but somehow it was always possible to wiggle or rationalize just enough to make things come out, or so I thought. Years later, usually after a conversation with some overly explicit line manager who found it necessary to remind me what idiots we HR people were, I began to plumb the murky depths of this "fair and consistent" idea a bit further. What I found was, well, in a word, bothersome.

Working principally at firms with an avowed desire to remain union-free provided regular feeding for the consistency side of this equation. Much of our work was guided by the then-prevailing dogma that suggested that the best way to remain union-free was to act like you already had one. Translation—treat everybody the same, no matter what.

One day, early in my career, I found my boss, the company's director of labor relations (where did we get those job titles anyhow?) going totally ballistic. He was a pretty cool character—hardened by the Marines and regular skirmishes with one union or another—so it was unusual to see him like this. I asked what was the matter. It seems that he had just encountered one of the company's co-founders, a guy named Henry, walking aimlessly through the office handing out $50 bills to long-service employees whom he recognized. Nothing terribly scientific or well-planned, just a guy trying to recognize those who had served faithfully for many years.

My boss, a guy named Lou, pulled the offending founder aside and pointed out that he couldn't just walk around the office singling out employees for these on-the-spot bonuses. After all, what he gave to one he must give to everybody. He must be consistent, because to do otherwise would reek of favoritism. Though he was very good at winning representation elections (and a great guy to work for), Lou had a habit of doing other things that pretty well guaranteed that he had reached the zenith of his career with the company. Telling a co-founder what he could and couldn't do with his money and his company was one of those things.

Henry's reaction was to 1) remind him of their respective rungs on the food chain and 2) give him a note that, when taken to the company's treasurer, would equip him with enough cash to similarly reward any (and every) employee who even dreamt of complaining about the disparate treatment. From that day on, with a special cylinder lock freshly installed on his office door, Lou kept a drawer full of fifties for such an occasion. (I am not making this up!) After all, even if the founder had been a little premature and unstructured in launching his version of the employee service award program, we were going to be consistent, by golly.

But was it fair? We think not. What's fair about rewarding a long-timer with $50, and then giving the same amount to a relative newcomer who simply threatens to complain? What's fair about giving a 4 out of 5 to all but the most egregiously poor performers on their annual performance evaluations? Consistent, perhaps. But grossly unfair.

We would argue that *consistency* means treating all people equally. *Fairness*, by contrast, means treating each individual *appropriately,* and *individually,* based on the circumstances, including the contribution of that individual. What he or she deserves or has earned, if you will.

What is "fair" anyhow? It depends on whom you ask, and what the circumstances are, doesn't it? Some would say that to be fair is to be just. Maybe. Go ask the client of, say, defense attorney Mark Geragos if he wants justice (fairness). Our bet is he'd opt for freedom over a scrupulously fair trial.

We looked the word up in the Webster's Collegiate Dictionary, 10th Edition. It didn't offer much help in resolving the question. On one hand it uses terms like impartial, honest, and free from self-interest. Then, it suggests that fairness is a matter of "conforming with the established rules" (however nonsensical they may be). We're starting to get, in addition to a headache, a pretty good idea where the "consistent" part of the doctrine came from. Since "fair" is so d*mned difficult to figure out, maybe we should just be consistent. It's *so* much easier. Just ask any parent who has at least two kids.

> *Nothing demotivates people like the equal treatment of unequals.*
> *When you hire a bozo and treat him the same as a rock star, it*
> *deflates the rock star.* —Joe Kraus, founder, Excite.com[1]

Fairness, then, depends on something external. Circumstances, situations, performance, contribution—something. Consistency, by definition, depends on nothing but conformity to an existing standard. Consistency requires good records. Fairness requires the application of good judgment. Kind of like discretionary effort.

This chapter has more than its share of words like "but," "however," and "still." Leading in a "fair" manner is rarely cut and dried, black and white. It calls for discernment and a degree of wisdom. While the passage of time affords these qualities the opportunity to develop in a person, they certainly are not reserved only for leaders with wrinkles and difficulty reading small print close up.

Still (see, we told you), it seems reasonable to say that people like (and deserve) to be treated with some element of consistency. Unless we're the ones on the receiving end of some undeserved preferential consideration, we get upset when, *under like circumstances*, we don't get treated like the next guy.

> Consistency requires good records. Fairness requires the application of good judgment.

UNDER LIKE CIRCUMSTANCES

If my neighbor and I are each doing 15 mph over the speed limit, and we each get pulled over for speeding, I'd like to believe that the ticket and fine we both get is the same. If I find that he got off and I was ticketed and fined $120, I may be happy for him, but I'm bothered by the lack of consistency. However, if I'm on the way to work and he's on the way to the nearest hospital, transporting his mother who is suffering chest pains, I can see my way around the fact that our circumstances are not the same.

So, what does any of this have to do with discretionary effort? Here's what: When, in pursuit of consistency, we abandon fairness, something happens to Oomph! It's like a slow leak in one of the tires on your car. Eventually, it becomes entirely deflated, or perhaps blows out altogether.

From the outset, we have held that the expenditure of discretionary effort is entirely a conscious decision. When someone makes that decision to Oomph! (a decision that distinguishes him from others), but then his effort is rewarded in an *undistinguished* manner (that is, with consistency rather than fairness), he will find it hard to sustain discretionary effort. Common reward for uncommon effort is a slap in the face.

A 3 percent across-the-board salary increase for everyone on your team is, in our view, *not* fair, unless you have observed an across-the-board improvement in performance, or are making market adjustments. What is

truly fair is a reward system based on the notion that distinguished performance merits distinguished reward.

The same is true for the opposite of rewards—sanctions or punishment.
To the degree that punishment is an effective "correction device" for adults,
it is foolhardy and just plain lazy to spray everyone in your group with the
same sanctions when it's clear that not everyone is guilty of whatever infrac-
tion is being dealt with. Yet it's a common practice. Two or three people begin
to demonstrate difficulty in distinguishing the company's time from their
own, and we clamp more restrictions on everyone. Those who are, in fact,
guilty, don't get the punishment they deserve; some of those who had been
scrupulous in their work habits before now begin to question why they were
so honest if they're going to be treated like everyone else.

Consider the use of the Internet as an example. Most reasonable people
would agree that occasionally accessing a benign Web site for personal

use while at work is natural these days, to be
expected, and of little harm to the employer.

Inevitably, someone will take undue advantage of the freedom to do these reasonable things
and spend hours downloading tunes to his MP3
player, booking a very involved set of vacation
plans, or gawking at salacious images online.
The organization could hardly be blamed for
wanting to put a stop to this kind of activity. But
the typical reaction is for someone in middle

When, in pursuit of consistency, we abandon fairness, something happens to Oomph!

management to execute an institutional response, administered and enforced
through further technological means, that restricts virtually all non-work-
related Internet access to everyone except those with the highest clearance.

Organizations whose leaders understand the benefits of fairness over
consistency might, instead, do the following:

- Be clear from day one that personal use of the company's Internet access
  is limited as to time, content, and activity. Those who require a more
  granular definition of those limits should either ask their manager to
  provide one or, after careful consideration of what they would consider
  appropriate, use their judgment. Or perhaps they shouldn't be there in
  the first place.

- Adopt a system that monitors Internet use on the employer's equipment. If something comes up that doesn't look right, deal with that

individual, and leave those who had nothing to do with it out of it. That's only—well—fair.

Trust . . . but verify. —Ronald Reagan

BALANCED WORTH-ITS

Discretionary effort seems to respond well to the notion of *quid pro quo*. I'll bend over backward, go out of my way, the extra mile—every idiom you can think of for Oomph!—if circumstances call for it. But, at some point, I'm going to expect an added measure of consideration from you.

And you means *you*. Not your company. Not your department, or some other entity that can hide behind institutional policies and norms. We said in chapter 1, "Work is contractual . . . effort is personal."

If I'm a CPA working for a tax accounting firm, I'll put in the thirteen hours a day during tax season, work every weekend, make special arrangements for the kids' transportation to and from school, and even skip my cousin's wedding in Nebraska. But, when the end of May rolls around, don't even *think* about saying anything when I want to go to the ceremony at 2:15 on a Tuesday afternoon to see my daughter get the school's math and science award.

The world of work is rife with managers (not leaders) whose sense of balance seems to be a little lopsided. The worker who arrives ten minutes late is subject to scrutiny and reprimand. But when the same worker stays an hour past quittin' time to participate in a conference call originating in another time zone, she has a right—if we're going to be fair about it—to expect a similar degree of scrutiny and, with it, at least a simple thank you.

Police Lt. Lindsay Boxer to Detective Warren Jacoby, in a discussion of a particularly tense murder investigation: I need you to work overtime.
Jacoby: Tonight?
Boxer: Unpaid overtime . . .
Jacoby: Aw, geez, Lieutenant, I just remembered . . . I got opera tickets.
Boxer: . . . because I've used up my overtime budget for the month. Because I don't have a bona fide victim. And because I don't even know what the hell this is.
Boxer, as narrator: Jacoby caved. Knowing I'd do the same for him.*

*From *The Fifth Horseman* by James Patterson and Maxine Paetro[2]

EARNING THE BENEFIT OF THE DOUBT

Err on the side of grace. —Bob Harvey, president
and CEO, Transcription Relief Services

To paraphrase a popular bumper sticker, "Stuff Happens." Drawbridges get stuck, alarm clocks with perfectly good track records fail, people lose their car keys, their babysitters don't show up, they have bad days, temporarily forget how to do something they mastered years ago, say things they don't mean, and, in short, are subject to all the foibles of being human. Just ask Mel Gibson. Leaders who are fair usually give people the benefit of the doubt. In return, they usually receive the benefit of the Oomph!

A good model for extending the benefit of the doubt comes from an interesting source: Netflix, the Los Gatos, California-based online DVD rental company. In the special circumstance of 2005's Hurricane Katrina, Netflix took proactive and enlightened steps to help customers affected by the storm who had a lot more to worry about than their DVD accounts. The company ascertained from the Postal Service the ZIP codes whose residents were not receiving mail, and notified each of them by e-mail that they could at least take Netflix off their list of concerns. Their accounts would be suspended until such time as the customer wished to resume the relationship. They needn't worry about items that may have been lost in transit, in either direction, or in the storm, and they wouldn't be charged the monthly fee until they wanted to start their service again.

Leaders who are fair usually give people the benefit of the doubt. In return, they usually receive the benefit of the Oomph!

According to Steve Swasey, the company's corporate communications director, replies flooded in from the affected customers, expressing appreciation for Netflix taking even this small step to be of help, and not add to their troubles. The irony of this wasn't lost on Netflix customers who were still getting power bills for electricity not delivered to uninhabitable or non-existent homes.

But this is how Netflix regards all its customers, even in ordinary circumstances. It's just the way they do business. The benefit of the doubt. Trust. The company's management understands that a DVD may occasionally be lost or damaged during shipping through no fault of the customer, even in good weather. Therefore, its policy is to replace lost movies at no charge. (In my case, the company was very understanding when my letter carrier delivered a Postal Service baggie containing shards of *Walk the Line,* with accompanying official USPS apology sticker, mass-produced expressly for such mishaps.)

However, the Netflix policy also states, "If an excessive number of lost DVD reports are filed on an account, we will place the account under review and notify the customer via e-mail." In other words, stuff happens. But don't confuse your stuff with our stuff.

We like the fact that their policy doesn't state a specific number of allowable losses. That game would be pretty easy to crack, wouldn't it? Instead, their policy operates from a foundation of trust, and extends to those who continue to earn that trust.

"We hire adults, and expect them to behave like adults."

The same practice works well with people at work. We start from a foundation of trust. If we've hired right, most of the people we've hired will enrich their trust account a little bit (sometimes a lot) each day. Then, when the drawbridge gets stuck, and they arrive later than usual, we barely remember. If the drawbridge gets stuck three times a week, a little coaching is probably in order.

As we suspected, Netflix's policy of trust with its customers also extends to its employees. "We hire adults, and expect them to behave like adults," said Swasey. This "we hire adults" attitude is particularly evident in Netflix's vacation policy, which is best defined by the fact that they *have* no vacation policy for their salaried workforce. (Production workers in their distribution facilities have a vacation policy that balances time off with customer demands.)

"Our policy is this," Swasey said, "as long as you get your work accomplished, take as much time as you want, whenever you want." Netflixers have to let their managers know when they're going to be gone—they don't have to ask permission—they simply need to let the bosses know, and then they are free to take vacation time at their own discretion. No one "vacates" during a big project or when a particular task is mission-critical. But when projects are completed, work is done, milestones are reached, Netflix says, "Take some vacation time if you want. And have a good time."

Steeped in a culture of two to three weeks *max* vacation at any given time, we asked Swasey, "What if someone wanted to take, like, a month or more at one time?"

"Oh, sometimes people take several months at a time. That's no problem," explained Swasey. We have a lot of software engineers and other professionals whose extended families live overseas. When they finish a big project, they go home to visit, sometimes for a couple of months or more. Plus, in our business, people can work online from almost anywhere. And our people do."

We should have known that Netflixers weren't taking undue advantage of the vacation non-policy. The company, with its simple and extremely well-executed business model, has one of the best-oiled distribution systems on the planet. It grew from nothing in 1999 to more than five million subscribers and $1 billion in revenue in 2006. Online customer service trackers ForeSee Results and FGI Research ranked it the number one Web site for customer service in 2004 and 2005, and *Fast Company* gave Netflix the magazine's 2005 Customers First Award.

But wait, there's more. Netflix has stayed well on top of its market, despite Blockbuster Video's attempts to capsize it. And, get this—Wal-Mart, not known for caving to competition, abandoned its short-lived try at the DVD rental business and told its customers to go to Netflix.

It would be hard to rack up successes like that with an AWOL workforce, or one that wasn't putting forth some pretty serious Oomph!

ACCOUNTING FOR PERSONAL CONSIDERATIONS

A manager's job would indeed be simpler if everyone had the same situations and circumstances, the same good fortune, and the same cast of characters at home. But, of course, they don't. And they never will.

Good people arrive in our application files in varying states of chronic and acute health. As their employment progresses with us, they get older, with all the physiological accompaniments of progressing from youth to middle age and beyond. They get sick, and then well. And then sick again. They bear children, lose loved ones, suffer property damage, enter and exit marriages, and move into new homes.

There's no denying that a forty-two-year-old single custodial father of three school-aged children is in a different place than a twenty-eight-year-old childless married woman, or a fifty-nine-year-old executive living on a golf course. So, some would ask, is it "fair" to treat these people differently?

That's a tough one. Really. The single parent in "survival mode" may simply have less to give at work than the exec with fewer demands on her time and energy outside of work, and yet both have jobs to do. And it's certainly fair to expect them to perform well at their respective jobs.

It's *not* fair to have different sets of standards for different people, but it *is* fair, and productive, to cut someone a break if they need it. The application of fairness, balanced with compassion and understanding, certainly results, in most cases, in the exertion of discretionary effort on the part of the person being given the break. It also reassures the people around them that, under like circumstances, they can probably expect the benefit of similar consideration.

> *It's not fair to have different sets of standards for different people, but it is fair, and productive, to cut someone a break if they need it.*

THERE'S ONE IN EVERY CROWD

Jan has worked for her company for twelve years and has an outstanding performance record and reputation with customers and colleagues alike. Her husband leaves her and, a few months later, her teenage son is seriously injured in a sports accident. He now requires around-the-clock care at home. The company changes insurance carriers, and the home-care provider she's been using isn't on the new plan. The red tape involved in securing another home-care provider results in a projected six-week gap in service for Jan's son. The core elements of Jan's job can be done via computer at home, although the company generally prefers people work at a central office location, for a variety of valid reasons. Under the circumstances, you, Jan's manager, go to some trouble and expense to make it possible for Jan to work at home for six weeks.

A sense of teamwork has flourished in your department over the course of the last couple of years, and all of Jan's co-workers support this plan. Several have volunteered to take paperwork by her house during this time, to save her trips to the office. Jan has come to the office for a few meetings during the time she's worked from home, having made arrangements, at her expense, for someone to be with her son for a few hours at a time.

While everyone Jan works with thinks the plan is not only fair, but far preferable to anything else for the time being, someone in the legal department thinks it would be better to investigate putting Jan on leave, via the Family Medical Leave Act.

The only other rumblings are from a guy named Tim, in another department. Tim's never been married, has no kids, and plans on keeping it that way. He has long resented all the "extra consideration" that parents get at work, pointing out, "We all make choices. It's too bad what happened to Jan's son, but, after all, no one made him join the football team. It doesn't seem fair that, just because you've decided to have kids, you get all the extra bennies." Tim doesn't see the twenty minutes a day he spends on smoke breaks in the parking lot as an extra bennie.

By the time the legal department finishes investigating the implications and possibilities of putting Jan on family medical leave, Jan—who is very appreciative of the consideration she's been shown by her manager—has been able to find a qualified caregiver, covered by the company's medical plan, and has returned to work at the office two weeks earlier than she had planned.

Jan's happy. The legal department is a little miffed. And Jan's attitude experiences an upgrade to Extra Miler status. Oomph!

Because the decision to part with discretionary effort is personal, so must be our consideration of individual workers if we are to expect them to make that decision in the organization's favor. Clearly, it would be easier to treat everyone with cookie-cutter-like consistency. But it would also probably be easier for your people to ugh, rather than Oomph! This isn't about being easy.

This isn't about being easy.

We're not suggesting that we, as leaders, get all balled up trying to do this for that one, and that for this one, flip-flopping on policies and standards. Our suggestions: Keep standards high, provide the means for people in varying circumstances to reach those standards, and engage compassion, judgment, and fairness. It will come back to you in spades.

CHAPTER SUMMARY

1. It is unfair to tolerate chronically poor performers and to keep them on the payroll. It's unfair to the poor performers, the good performers, your customers, and your shareholders.
2. Good leaders treat people with fairness, not because of laws, but because it makes sense and produces better results.
3. Fairness is not the same as consistency. Consistency means treating all people the same; fairness means treating them appropriately and individually, based on the circumstances, balanced with a degree of compassion.
4. Oomph! responds to the concept of "balanced worth-its." Most people are happy to give it all they've got, as long as someone cuts them a break when they need it.
5. Leaders can demonstrate fairness by extending the benefit of the doubt, until and unless given a good reason not to.
6. Few areas call for fairness more than that of work/life balance.

MONDAY MORNING, 8AM

1. If there's someone under your leadership who has lost the right to keep working in your organization, stop ignoring or tolerating it. If you've provided the person useful and meaningful feedback and opportunities to rehabilitate his or her employment, and he or she is still underperforming, sever the relationship as soon as possible. Do it humanely and respectfully, but do it.

2. Evaluate the way you treat those you lead on the basis of fairness . . . and consistency. If your consistency has compromised your fairness, take steps to shift the emphasis back toward fairness.

15

A LEADER SETS THE BAR HIGH

*The truth of the matter is that you always know the
right thing to do. The hard part is doing it.*
— General H. Norman Schwarzkopf, U.S. Army, ret.

No one gets up in the morning and says, "I want to get beat today—I want
to go lose, to hang out with a bunch of really mediocre people." Internally,
we all feel a drive to win, to be successful. Granted, each of us has a different
definition and barometer of success, but it is there.

Indeed, the prospect of winning (or maybe it is the fear of losing) often
provides the spark that ignites our passion. Ask someone what winning
means to them, or have them tell you about a point in time when they were
part of a winning team or effort, and you will see their eyes immediately light
up. Ask them a second question, "What is it like to lose?" Or have them tell
you about a time when they lost. That twinkle in the eye goes away, just as
fast as it appeared.

As the result of that inner desire, most of us seem to understand innately
that achieving success requires real work and sacrifice. Indeed, deep down,
we seem to "get it" that winning requires some standards of conduct or
behavior—high standards in fact. We don't always perform to those standards, but we understand the deal.

Extra Miler: SFC Jim Lusk—In October 2004, Sgt. 1st Class Jim Lusk led a platoon of soldiers from the Army's Stryker Brigade into battle in Iraq. By virtue of prior service in the first Gulf War, Sgt. Lusk was not required to deploy on this mission, but out of a sense of duty to his troops, his country, and his profession, he took the high road and joined the platoon on their journey into harm's way. Learning of the sergeant's selfless decision, we took a special interest in him, his platoon, and their activities and accomplishments in Iraq.

Deep down, we seem to "get it" that winning requires some standards of conduct or behavior—high standards in fact.

After completing an eleven-month tour that consisted of violent, daily, up-close and personal skirmishes with both foreign fighters and Iraqi insurgents in places like Mosul, Fallujah, and Tal Afar, Sergeant Lusk returned to Fort Lewis, Washington, in September 2005, bringing with him each and every one of the young men he had led into battle.

Figuring that we could learn a thing or two from the sergeant, we queried him about his views on leadership. With the clear, crisp, no-nonsense point of view one gets from a hardened combat veteran, he didn't disappoint. Some of his words about performance and high standards follow.

> Give your subordinates a sense of pride in themselves and their unit by assigning them tough, but realistic and attainable, goals. This fosters great esprit de corps and sets the stage for them to accomplish astounding results.
>
> In training, I never let a soldier just quit and get on a truck. If a soldier thought they couldn't make it any more and wanted to give up, we would strap them in a SKEDKO, (a thick plastic sheet used to evacuate casualties from the battlefield) and drag them along until we reached the finish point. This is very labor-intensive—it takes two soldiers to drag one soldier along, plus two more to carry the wounded soldier's gear. Soldiers had to rotate out every five minutes or so. This training reinforced the creed of never leaving a comrade behind.
>
> As a leader, I would always attempt to take my turns pulling the SKEDKO, but was always told by my subordinates that it was their job to do that. It made me proud of them that they would not let

me pull it, it made them proud to accomplish a very tough and demanding job, and it made the soldier being evacuated never want to give up again and cause his comrades to have to give so much of themselves in order to get him to the objective.

TALENT MAGNETS

In the world of team sports, there are coaches who stand out because of their commitment to winning—people such as Pat Riley, Phil Jackson, Pat Summitt, Don Shula, Joe Torre, Vince Lombardi, Joe Gibbs, Bob Knight, Bill Parcells, Mike Krzyzewski, and John Wooden.

Over time, the most talented players in each sport have queued up to play for these coaches. And when they did, they had a very good sense of what they were signing up for. Usually, such players would have "star status" conferred on them on day one anywhere else, but not with these coaches, because by and large, they don't allow a "star system" to exist. Miami Heat coach Pat Riley put it best when he said, "Being a part of success is more important than being personally indispensable." In other words, it's about "team," not "me."

In many cases, some of these athletes might have made more money or gotten a softer deal playing somewhere else, but they chose not to because they wanted to be part of a winning organization. As a case in point, why would NFL quarterback Brett Favre want to practice his craft for a minor market team in Green Bay, Wisconsin, a place so cold that its field is referred to as the "frozen tundra?" We suspect the presence of a winning tradition has a lot to do with it.

Each of these coaches has exceptionally high standards—for their players and staff, the officials who referee their games, and for themselves.

Since 1963, Bob Knight has been coaching men's college basketball at places such as the U.S. Military Academy at West Point, Indiana University, and Texas Tech University. In that time, his teams have amassed over eight hundred wins and three NCAA championships, making him "one of the winningest coaches in basketball history."[1]

Fairly or otherwise, Coach Knight has also garnered a reputation for being—how shall we put this—extremely demonstrative when he wants to make a point. In some cases, the coach's rather explicit mode of communicating has gotten him in trouble. While we have no interest in being apologists for bad behavior, there seems little doubt that his passion for seeing kids learn and excel has a lot to do with an occasional profane rant or outburst.

In 2003, after a winning 16/11 season that the students, athletic director, and college president were all more than satisfied with, Coach Knight refused to accept his $250,000 paycheck from Texas Tech University. Commenting on the matter, he said, "When I was a kid, I used to shovel walks and do all kinds of stuff to make a dollar. But if I shoveled the walk, I made damn sure that I did a good job. I'm just not at all satisfied with what transpired with our team in terms of our fundamental execution. I don't think it's anybody's fault but mine."[2]

Leaders who refuse to exempt themselves from the strict accountability they impose on others usually achieve more.

"He has standards," men's basketball spokesman Randy Farley said. "He just didn't meet his standards, and so he said, 'I don't think I should be paid for that.'"[3] Our view is that leaders who refuse to exempt themselves from the strict accountability they impose on others usually achieve more.

IS GOOD ENOUGH GOOD ENOUGH?

> *Everyone tries to cross the fence where*
> *it is lowest.*   —Danish proverb

Somewhere along the way, the words "good enough" worked their way into our lexicon. Though it is likely they have always been there, our tolerance for their application seems to have increased exponentially and engendered a certain mindset. Sadly, in many respects, whether the standards are personal or organizational, we just don't have very high expectations anymore, particularly when it comes to personal and organizational behavior.

Be it in sports, politics, business, or everyday life, we seem to have reached an accommodation whereby the end always justifies the means. Whether it's steroid-amped baseball players using corked bats; so-called accountants at Enron, WorldCom, and others cooking the books; everybody with an MP3

We just don't have very high expectations anymore, particularly when it comes to personal and organizational behavior.

player toting a library of stolen music; students knocking off term papers; or residents of the White House lying to the nation, their spouses, or both; cheating is not only prevalent, it is commonly accepted. There doesn't even appear to be any shame.

As New York State attorney general, Eliot Spitzer made a living (not to mention a reputation) going after some of the companies and individuals involved in corporate shenanigans and, although he collected billions in fines from settlements, *practically no one went to jail.* (Except for Martha Stewart, one of the few remaining legal residents of America who doesn't mind cooking and cleaning. To her credit, she stepped up to the plate and took her medicine without whining, dodging, or dying.)

Contrary to the way it may seem, our approach to this issue is not on a moral plane, but a practical one. When we set modest standards and expectations, that is exactly what we get. Moreover, our study of high-performance organizations over the last decade suggests strongly that people dislike losing, and just don't like "hanging around with turkeys." At the water cooler, we whine and moan about high standards and expectations, but at the end of the day, we appreciate them, because we know intuitively that they are a necessary precursor to winning. Hence, high expectations, accompanied by ambitious goals, are a fundamental factor in tapping into the wellspring of discretionary effort.

At the water cooler, we whine and moan about high standards and expectations, but at the end of the day, we appreciate them, because we know intuitively that they are a necessary precursor to winning.

Josh Weston, former CEO and president of Automatic Data Processing, Inc., was fond of saying that he "would rather attempt a goal of climbing four stairs and accomplish only three, than to only attempt two in the first place." Having worked for the man for nearly five years, I can vouch for the fact that he gave (and got) a full measure of effort. And yes, despite the fact that he was a tough guy to please, if you had set the bar high, given it your best, and still come up a little short, he made it a point to let you know that he appreciated the effort. Climb on.

> *Most people have the will to win. Few have the will to prepare to win.*   —Coach Bob Knight

CHAPTER SUMMARY

1. High standards are a necessary precursor to high performance and winning. You get what you expect to get.
2. People will respect and appreciate high standards a lot more when they see their leaders subjecting themselves to the same (or greater) standard.
3. People want to work where there are high standards in place, and where they have a better-than-even chance of winning.

MONDAY MORNING, 8AM

1. Yes, we know it's morning, and you just spent time getting your "face on," but take another hard look in the mirror. Are you setting and keeping high standards? Really? Does it start with you?

2. There is a wonderful little video entitled *Brain Power*, starring John Houseman. It really makes the point about great expectations begetting high performance. We use it to launch senior management retreats. Get a copy.[4]

LEADERSHIP IS MORE THAN GETTING PEOPLE TO DRINK THE KOOL-AID

Leadership is the art of getting someone else to do something you want done, because he wants to do it.   —Dwight David Eisenhower

Extra effort is not necessarily *discretionary* effort. How can you tell the difference? And yes, before you ask, it *does* matter. You may observe extra effort—but not discretionary effort—occurring as the result of one or more of the following factors: fear; bullying, deceit, or humiliation; or a new standard or level of expectation.

Fear. I was once in a meeting with a group of training managers when the question was asked, "How do you determine if something is a training issue, or a motivational issue?" The senior member of the group, the training director for a large public utility, opined that if a person could perform the task with a gun held to his head, it was not a training issue. While his comment rankled the sensitivities of a few in the room, the old guy had a point. No pun intended.

Extra *effort is not necessarily* discretionary *effort.*

In the same way, if a degree of extra effort flows from a fear of consequences associated with withholding that extra effort, we can hardly say that the effort is discretionary.

There are any number of sanctions, official and de facto, that may be imposed on someone whose output (or input) doesn't regularly reach a certain level. I once worked for a company where the unspoken rule was to work eleven-hour days every day, or they'd find someone willing to do so. We all worked eleven-hour days, but the extra effort wasn't discretionary. Truth be told, we were present for eleven hours per day. Whether or not any more work got done is debatable.

Organizations have devised all manner of punishment designed to coerce just about any kind of behavior they want from people. Threats of termination, stagnant pay, poor evaluations, a cut in hours for those who are paid by the hour, and less-than-desirable projects are but a few of the ways we may obtain extra effort from people, for a time. But never discretionary effort.

In 1977, Jim Jones, a "minister" who had worn out his welcome in the United States because of his radical views and behavior, moved his "church," The People's Temple, to Guyana, South America, and created his dream community, Jonestown. The following year, Jonestown received a visit from U.S. Representative Leo Ryan, who was purportedly investigating human rights abuses within the community.

As Ryan's delegation was about to leave Guyana, the increasingly paranoid Jones, fearful that Ryan might tell the world what he had seen, had his security forces (since when does a church need those?) kill the congressman and the members of his delegation.

Then, for reasons not ever fully understood, Jones convinced his followers, all 913 of them, that it was time to end their lives and leave the earth. Most appear to have committed suicide by drinking a grape drink (rumored to be Kool-Aid) laced with cyanide and sedatives, including liquid Valium, Penegram, and chloral hydrate.

In the name of religion, Osama bin Laden has convinced thousands of followers, most notably the nineteen young men who hijacked and crashed four U.S.-flagged airplanes on September 11, 2001, to die for his cause.

There is nothing at all wrong with convincing an extremely loyal and motivated group of followers that they can do incredible things, and then helping them accomplish those aims. It is a far different matter, though, to misuse power for sinister purposes, to prey on the weak, or to use peoples' fears (or promise of ridiculous rewards, for example, an encounter with scores of virgins) to manipulate them, as Jones, bin Laden, Hitler, and others have done.

Very high-performance organizations (IBM in its early days, FedEx, Apple Computer, Microsoft, the U.S. Marines) tend to be home to a lot of discretionary effort, and indeed, often have what can legitimately be described as a cult-like following that includes insiders and outsiders alike.

These organizations can usually be characterized as being proud (think swagger), somewhat insular, headstrong about their way of doing things, and demanding of themselves and others, and they tend to be guided by visionary leaders with extraordinary communication skills. They usually have a very distinctive brand, which they leverage and seek to maintain, which is all well and good.

True discretionary effort cannot, by definition, be caused by bullying, intimidation, or humiliation.

They do not, however, gain or retain followers by means of coercion or deceit. Bill Gates, for example, may have used strong-arm tactics to blunt the thrusts of his competitors, but there doesn't seem to be any evidence to suggest that Microsoft employees have been coerced or hoodwinked. Consistent with our central premise, true discretionary effort cannot, by definition, be caused by bullying, intimidation, or humiliation.

Bullying, intimidation, or humiliation. A headline in the August 16, 2005 issue of the *Glasgow (Scotland) Herald* read: "Bank's food fight grows: Cauliflower replaces cabbage."[1]

The article, by chief reporter Iain Wilson, related the practice among managers at certain branches of the Bank of Scotland to use large-headed vegetables as motivational tools for the employees whose sales figures didn't quite cut the haggis.

Here's the deal: Fail to reach pre-determined goals for sales of bank accounts, insurance policies, and other services, and get a cabbage on your desk (or in some cases a cauliflower) as a badge of shame until it can be passed along to a colleague with even poorer results.

What a goofy idea. And apparently, Amicus, the British banking union, felt the same way. Management issued a series of apologies, and the practice went back to the cabbage patch. No one ever shamed discretionary effort out of anyone. Oomph! is when people, on their own initiative, get off the bench and into the game.

A new standard or level of expectation. A new, externally determined sales or productivity goal; some new method or procedure; a new requirement, policy, or government regulation. Introduce any of these (or other) stimuli, and you may see an additional increment of effort expended, but that doesn't necessarily mean that it is discretionary effort.

For example, have you noticed that in just about every retail establishment you walk into these days, the minute you get within ten feet of a store employee, that person stops, smiles, says hello, and often inquires about your health? That didn't used to happen. OK, it did when our parents were young, but it hasn't happened for a long time. Is this new phenomenon the result of discretionary effort? Or

No one ever shamed discretionary effort out of anyone.

is it because someone has gone around the country making a boatload of money training retail employees to smile and acknowledge every customer in the store as a way of increasing sales? We suspect the latter. Our cynicism, however, could be wrong if, in fact, that employee does more than barely part his lips, and actually *means* to convey a measure of goodwill.

In similar fashion, a common practice in the casual dining business is for restaurant managers to walk around the restaurant and check in with guests to make sure their dining experience is going well, a practice referred to in the trade as "touching tables." If a manager never did that before, but now, as a result of a new corporate practice, she does it routinely, thereby requiring extra effort on her part, is she, or is she not, expending discretionary effort? For some, it may be discretionary effort. For most, however, it is simply a matter of complying with a new procedure—conforming to a new standard—that happens to require a change in behavior.

You're a salesman. Your sales quota was $800,000 in year A. You reached and slightly exceeded your quota, and your new quota for year B is $1 million. That takes more work, more effort, and that additional effort appears to be responsible for your reaching and slightly exceeding the new goal. Was that discretionary effort? We think not. If, however, your goal for year C remains at $1 million, and you reached $1.4 million, that may be—repeat, *may* be—a result of discretionary effort. Especially if you took it upon yourself to make five additional sales calls a day, attend additional sales training, read three new books on successful selling, and set the alarm clock thirty minutes earlier every morning than you did in years A and B.

Suppose your manager retires and you get a new boss. Her arrival is accompanied by a sense of a new beginning, and expectations are high that she will breathe new life into a department that has become complacent with mediocrity. You're keen to impress her, so you kick it into overdrive. Is *that* discretionary effort? You bet it is!

Now, the question turns to what happens next in this scenario. You have made a choice to put more effort into what you do, to go above and beyond what has been expected, because you feel a new chapter has begun in your work. Your new manager now has a choice to make, and an opportunity. She may either keep the Oomph! valve open, causing you to part with discretionary effort as a matter of course. Or she may choose to take measures that will—*whether this is her intention or not*—stop the flow of Oomph! on your part.

SO WHAT?

Our point is this: Discretionary effort is a conscious choice. It is discretionary. Fear removes that choice. New procedures, requirements, regulations, goals, and expectations give rise to new behaviors that do not necessarily qualify as Oomph! But when a person chooses to go above and beyond, not because they have to, but because they want to—*that's* Oomph! Why does it matter? Because that which is freely given stands a much better chance of lasting without artificial stimuli. Just as it is only the individual who can turn it on, only the individual can turn it off.

> *Discretionary effort is a conscious choice. It is discretionary. Fear removes that choice.*

CHAPTER SUMMARY

1. Extra effort is not necessarily discretionary effort.

2. Discretionary effort is just that—discretionary. Effort that comes as the result of threats or coercion will vanish the instant the sanctions are removed.

3. By the same token, effort driven by changes in expectations, rules, policies, or outside influences may not constitute discretionary effort. This is more than semantics. Discretionary effort is, by definition, voluntary. Only the individual can turn it on, and only the individual can turn it off.

MONDAY MORNING, 8AM

1. Take a hard look at the managers in your organization and answer the question, "Who is getting results, albeit short-lived, through coercion and intimidation, and who is getting real Oomph!?"

2. Take stock of some of the signs of Oomph! in your organization. Do you see some of the swagger, are people sweating and smiling at the same time, are your standards high enough?

SECTION FIVE

OOMPH! PROCESSES

IT'S THE PROCESS, STUPID!

Ninety percent of what we call "management" consists of making it difficult for people to get things done. —Peter Drucker

Things aren't always as they seem. If it looks like the people around you aren't giving their all, maybe they are, but their all isn't getting through. It's being blocked or frustrated by some of the processes, rules, policies, habits, norms, and traditions that have grown up like garden weeds in the workplace. Like a car with underinflated tires, energy is going into their work, but it's getting sucked up by the inefficiencies and frustrations—some minor, others major—that stand in their way.

Leaders who get more Oomph! from their people are diligent about monitoring and, when possible, changing and eliminating processes that get in the way of discretionary effort. And beyond just eliminating obstacles, they build in systems that grease the skids and make it easier for people to get things done. This is really about setting people free—freeing them up to do their very best work. So often, we project a goal, then put structures in place that practically guarantee a shortfall. We frustrate people by keeping them from doing their best work and, if they do manage to reach the goal, they've often had to burn more fuel than the journey was worth.

> *This is really about setting people free—freeing them up to do their very best work.*

We've observed, in the best leaders, a relentless brutality in changing and eliminating systems and processes that just don't work. They have no pride of authorship in a rule that has outlived its usefulness (if it ever had any).

When speaking to management groups, we often challenge audience members to write down one utterly stupid process, rule, or system in their *own* area that hampers the flawless execution of their mission. Many are at a loss to produce even one candidate. To these, we say, "If you can't think of anything, go back and ask your employees. They'll tell you more than you want to know." We're not kidding.

Several years ago, I bought tickets over the phone for my wife and me to attend a concert at the brand-new University of North Florida Fine Arts Center. We were eager to experience the state-of-the-art performance venue, as well as the artists, Three Mo' Tenors, a trio whose repertoire includes everything from classical to gospel to pop.

As we entered the UNF campus, we joined a long, slow-moving queue approaching a tiny booth from which a student dispensed parking passes, at $3 a pop. I didn't mind paying a dollar an hour to rent a plot of valuable Florida real estate for my car to occupy during the performance, but the twenty-minute wait in the queue was aggravating. We got the pass, parked, and entered the beautiful theatre, rushed and harried, just five minutes before curtain time. It was half-empty, for a show we'd heard was sold out.

The rest of the audience was waiting in line to pay for parking. Horns were blaring, the kid in the booth (reaffirming his decision to seek higher education) was ready to abandon his post, and the theatre staff (volunteers all) were enduring the bitter complaints of every patron—as if they were the ones responsible for formulating campus parking policy. Nearly a half-hour after curtain time, once a quorum had assembled, the concert commenced.

The next day, I wrote a letter to Sharon Papian, executive director of the Fine Arts Center, telling her how impressed we had been both with the artists and the beautiful facility. However, I suggested, the parking pass issue was big and ugly enough to make me think twice about making a return visit. I suspected I wasn't alone in that thought and, if that were the case, the UNF Fine Arts Center would have more struggles than it needed in its inaugural season.

I passed along a suggestion that, since we had given our credit card number for the tickets, and they were mailing the tickets to our home, why not tack an extra three bucks onto the bill and include a parking pass with the tickets?

The day after that (the Postal Service was operating at peak efficiency, I suppose), I got a call from Ms. Papian, thanking me for my input and inviting me to sit on the Fine Arts Center's Board, an invitation I accepted.

She didn't do the bureaucratic thing (this is, after all, a state university) and rattle off all the reasons they couldn't possibly implement my suggestion. Instead, in the spirit of continuous improvement, Sharon made a few phone calls to equally sensible members of the university's administration, and the plan was put in place.

Two shows later (remember, this *is* a state university), with the parking pass plan implemented, the booth queue consisted solely of will-calls and walkups, a small portion of the overall audience. And the show started on time. The kid in the booth had a better evening. He got more studying done. The pages and ushers stopped wondering what they had gotten themselves into. Sharon Papian received no letters complaining about parking. The performance started and finished on time. The artists got enough sleep before busing to the next city on their tour, no doubt able to put more Oomph! into their next performance.

All because somebody fixed the system!

> *The keystone of successful business is cooperation. Friction*
> *retards progress.*   —James Cash Penney, founder, J. C. Penney Co.

COOPERATION IS MORE THAN GETTING ALONG

While organizational leaders espouse the value of cooperation, often their processes encourage the opposite, resulting in systemic blockage of Oomph! One of the experiential activities we often use in leadership seminars brings to light just how powerful our incentives *not to cooperate* in any way can be. This activity operates on a simple premise and with easy-to-understand instructions. Without giving away the entire plot, we'll just tell you that in each of ten rounds, four teams are asked to make one choice between two possible courses of action. On its face, neither course of action is any better or worse than the other. It is the *combination* of choices made by the collection of the four teams that determines each group's reward, or penalty. Stick with me on this.

Each team's choice is independent of all other teams' choices and, at first, the teams are not permitted to communicate with each other. With the payoff schedule for every possible combination of the four teams' choices projected in living color on a screen, the clear, obvious, and undisputed reality is that if every team goes with choice A, all will profit. The term "no-brainer" was coined precisely for this type of decision.

However, a seductive option exists for any team to double or even triple their payoff potential if *they* go with B and at least one other team takes the high road to A. Predictably, in all but a few cases, most teams have *knowingly* selected the choice that guarantees a loss. While the win-win-win-win scenario is clearly placed before them, the *rules of the game* make it a nearly sure bet that greed and selfishness will prevail, awarding the winnings to the house, not to the players.

Even after we relax the rules and let the teams collude, somebody still picks B. It happens every time. Why? The process effectively makes the prospect of competition look, deceivingly, far more attractive than that of cooperation. Not unlike, we suspect, the way it works in your organization.

> *Only strength can cooperate. Weakness can*
> *only beg.* —Dwight David Eisenhower

JOB SWAP?

The case for emulating Southwest Airlines is strong. Since its first flight in 1971, this low-fare, low-cost, and low-pretension carrier has yet to fail to have a profitable year. After 2001, when all its domestic competitors were gushing red ink, whining unendingly, shamelessly taking unearned and undeserved government support, and then bailing under bankruptcy, Southwest remained at the top of a very short list of well-performing airlines, in the eyes of its customers, employees, and shareholders.

Southwest owes its success to many factors, among them low-cost practices, fuel hedging, and probably a little good luck. But no other factor can claim as much of the credit for this airline's success as its people practices. It's not just the way they treat their employees, but the entire way they think about them and, in turn, the processes that have emerged.

To be sure, Southwest is not everyone's favorite airline. Many of our pampered friends, colleagues, and competitors decry the cattle-car mentality that pervades the boarding process. Others miss the frills of the full-service carriers (although we're perplexed as to what those frills are). Still, every process, procedure, policy, habit, and tradition that drives the daily operation

The rules of the game *make it a nearly sure bet that greed and selfishness will prevail.*

at Southwest is designed to optimize what they know to be most important to *their* market (getting from place A to place B safely, reliably, and affordably), and still make an attractive profit for their investors.

I once noticed, on a Southwest flight, a male flight attendant who didn't quite fit the mold. He was a little older, fit less comfortably into the flight attendant's casual uniform, and, frankly, was less sure of his actions than his co-workers were. During the post-peanut lull that ensues between New Orleans and Phoenix, I had a chance to engage the man in conversation. I like to talk to people who work for companies with distinguished workplace reputations, to find out whether the experience is more a product of reality than the PR engine.

"How do you like working for Southwest?" I inquired.

"I love it!" The enthusiasm was genuine.

"How long have you been with the company?" I asked, catching myself sounding more like a reporter than an interested passenger.

"Seventeen years," he said.

A little surprised that his reply was seventeen years and not seventeen days, all I could think was "Nice guy . . . but slow learner." Without stopping to edit my surprise, I responded, "Really? As a flight attendant?"

Without stopping to edit his response to what he knew I was thinking, he said, "I'm not a flight attendant. I'm a pilot. A couple of times a year, we each come back here to work with the folks who *really* keep this plane in the air."

After thinking, "How cool is that?" my next question was, "This isn't like a job-trade thing, is it?" He assured me that it was not, and that in fact there were two fully qualified pilots on the flight deck, a third passing out peanuts and drinks, and a fourth in the center seat in row 25.

The chapters that follow in this section deal with processes like this and others—internal and external—that have an impact on discretionary effort. Designed one way, each has the power to liberate discretionary effort from every member of your workforce; designed in other ways (or not designed at all), they can frustrate any hope of Oomph!

As you read these next two chapters, consider your role in unleashing discretionary effort in your outfit, by making sure the systems support its expenditure, not thwart it.

CHAPTER SUMMARY

1. Processes (communication, decision-making, cooperation, and customer service) drive or diminish discretionary effort.
2. Good leaders monitor and adjust work processes to get the maximum Oomph! from people.

MONDAY MORNING, 8AM

1. Ask three or four people you work with to tell you the *one* dumbest policy under which they work. Tell them you want to hear about the real stinkers.

2. If more than one person cites the same item, assume they might have a point. Figure out who "owns" it, and get it fixed.

3. Undoubtedly you're working on several major projects or initiatives with colleagues right now. For at least one of those projects, look for ways to cooperate with those colleagues in a way that doesn't benefit you directly, but that benefits the organization.

4. Determine one system or process currently under your control that impedes cooperation among team members or various parts of your organization. Change the system so that it accomplishes the same objective, while enabling greater cooperation.

18

A LEADER MAKES MEANING

Keep your mouth shut. Best way to handle them (buffalo) is to put some duct tape over your mouth. If they get excited, they'll get lost or get away, you'll scare them. Duct tape is a good investment. —Ray O. Smith, buffalo rancher[1]

It seems unarguable that, in the twenty-first century, we have more communication tools at our disposal than ever before. Darned near everyone in the civilized world is tethered to a cellphone, PDA, or laptop, used almost incessantly to talk to people, either by voice or text messages. With the advent of the iPod and other MP3 devices, "podcasts" are created and disseminated like popcorn at a theater on a busy Friday night.

Likewise, corporate communications budgets have never been more robust. Aside from all the gear, we have more communication strategists, media specialists, and spinmeisters than you can shake a stick at. Yet it seems fair to say that we do a poorer job of communicating than perhaps at any time in history. Communicating—as in conversing, exchanging views, building commitment, making meaning.

Don't get us wrong. We are not technophobes—anything but. In fact, we tend to be rather early adopters of new technology in our business and personal lives. But it's important—no, imperative—to understand that technology does not make meaning . . . people do! And making meaning is what communicating is all about. It is what leaders do.

We do a substantial amount of our work in the healthcare field and, accordingly, we value any opportunity to do field research. A few years ago, I had the occasion to spend time in what is unquestionably one of the finest heart hospitals in the southwestern United States—a shiny, new facility with state-of-the-art everything. It wasn't a scheduled visit. Instead, after mysteriously passing out and clobbering the floor of my hotel room with my head, I arrived at the hospital horizontally in the middle of the night, accompanied by two crews of EMTs.

> *It's important —no, imperative—to understand that technology does not make meaning . . . people do! And making meaning is what communicating is all about.*

I was wheeled into room 4 and descended upon by an RN, nurse technician, and soon, the on-duty ER physician. Each was polite, professional, and focused on doing his or her job. After the administration of IV fluids and an assortment of drugs, my heart decided to convert from atrial fib to normal sinus rhythm on its own.

Over the next thirty-six hours, I had a whole bunch of tests run to see what kind of damage can be done by the combination of atrial fibrillation and using one's head as a pile driver. In the process, I also got to observe the internal workings of a hospital—something I hadn't done since my college days when I worked as an orderly.

SOME OBSERVATIONS

1. Numerous medical professionals have suggested that when it comes to healthcare, there are four key components: patients, caregivers, science/technology, and money. I would propose a fifth—information, specifically its capture, use, and dissemination. Sadly, in my experience, the information handling (or lack thereof) within the hospital essentially mitigated any advantages of having a wonderful facility and a trained, motivated staff. For that matter, it's likely true of *all* our businesses, not just healthcare.

There is simply no reason in the twenty-first century for professional staff (or any staff, for that matter) to have to ask patients (or customers) two or more times to supply their address, phone number, insurance ID, next of kin, family physician's name, and social security number, and record it on yet one more stinking form. If identity thieves can get all this and more from a few keystrokes on a computer, there has to be a better way to handle this process.

Lest we forget, this type of waste doesn't just interfere with patient care; it saps the morale of people who are smart enough to know that what they are doing at that moment is redundant and completely useless. As one RN pointed out to me, "I attended nursing school to put my hands on patients, not paper, and yet I now spend twenty-seven minutes of every hour feeding an overweight bureaucracy." And we wonder why so many nursing professionals are abandoning work they love because they hate their jobs!

2. Of greater concern is the fact that information flow within much of the healthcare organization is entirely one-way (all intake). The fact that I was never officially apprised of any test results during twenty-eight hours of nonstop testing and observation was more than a little bothersome. Sporting a portable heart monitor, I spent a morning on a lovely outdoor patio just outside my room retrieving e-mail via a Blackberry, while considerably more important stuff—namely, the results of an echocardiogram, CT scan, VQ scan, X-rays, and assorted blood tests—were seemingly lost within that very building!

There is simply no reason in the twenty-first century to have to ask patients or customers two or more times to supply their address, phone number, insurance ID, and social security number, and record it on yet one more stinking form.

Were it not for the kindness of technicians who could generally be coaxed to provide an unofficial "nod or wink" in response to questions about the results, I would have known nothing about my condition during this period. If you want to watch someone's heart rate and blood pressure go up needlessly, just keep them in the dark about their condition. In fact, when I finally *did* see somebody with an MD after their name, I suggested that this treatment might prove an effective, not to mention cheaper, alternative to the cardiac stress test.

I'd like to throw down the gauntlet for the medical community on this one. If FedEx can come to your door in the evening, pick up a package, and deliver it halfway around the world the very next morning for one-fourth the cost of a chest X-ray, is there really any valid reason why something at least approaching that standard of performance can't be achieved when it comes to acquainting anxious patients (and caregivers) with test results, and helping them understand them? Come on, folks!

3. As one who spends and depends heavily on technology to do his work, I'm about the last person to resist the sensible deployment of chips and software in the medical arena. But there must be limits. When an MD responsible for ordering tests and meds for a patient relies exclusively on remote digital data without the benefit of having seen, met, talked with, or examined that patient, it would seem that we have crossed into the danger zone. To be sure, there are cases when such methods are necessary, especially those involving the emergency rescue and transport of patients, but as a wise ER doc explained to me recently, the digitization of medicine is not entirely a good thing.

Ditto for the communications methods employed by the rest of us. E-mail, for example, is a wonderful creation. It's lightning-fast and free. But it's also only two-dimensional, and black and white. It's difficult, for example, to ascertain what people are NOT saying in an e-mail message. You get no chance to observe their body language or look them in the eye. To be sure, neither party can gauge the level of commitment associated with something said in an e-mail. For this reason, we steadfastly maintain that doing a performance review or heavy coaching session via e-mail (or telephone) is profoundly absurd.

> *Leaders don't just make products and make decisions.*
> *Leaders make meaning.* —John Seeley Brown,
> former chief scientist, Xerox Corporation

THE BASICS

At work, people—all of us—have some basic information needs that must be met as a condition of being competent and reasonably well-directed, if not hitting on all cylinders. In baseball parlance, this is first base. We need to know:

1. What's it like around here?
2. Where are we going?
3. How are we going to get there?
4. How do I fit in? What's my part?
5. How do I do this?
6. Why can't we do something? (when things are all screwed up)
7. How can I help?
8. What's in it for me?
9. Does anybody care?
10. How am I doing?

If we don't get clear, sensible, timely answers to these questions, and get them in a form that is digestible by our own unique learning style, we are incapable of doing very much at all, let alone performing with Oomph! It is akin to swimming with an anchor tied to your leg—a definite Oomph! buster. People who are already disinclined to part with any discretionary effort won't mind so much, but those who are more willing to give it up will be really annoyed.

A lot of our problems with communicating relate back to the aforementioned blizzard of messages. It gets in the way, dulls the senses. We've all become so inured to the cacophony of messages being beamed at us that we spend much of our waking time with our shields up and our receptors turned down, if not off. So what to do?

1. **Turn down the volume.** That's right—down, not up. It is impossible to compete with the roar that assaults everyone's ears, so don't try. Turn down the volume to be noticed.

2. **Communicate *with* people, not *at* them.** Once again, as Pebble Beach Company's Hubert Allen put it, it's personal. Let people know early on that their interests are every bit as important to you as the organization's, and even your own.

   While writing this piece, I was at a gate awaiting a flight at the Minneapolis–St. Paul airport. A Chicago flight was being boarded at an adjacent gate, and the gate agent had already made three boarding announcements and herded nearly everyone onto the plane. A few stragglers remained in the gate area, including a young woman who was listening intently to someone on her cellphone and sobbing noticeably.

Turn down the volume to be noticed.

   The agent approached the woman and admonished her to board the plane before it left. A couple minutes later, he returned to repeat the warning, this time a little more sternly. As her sobbing had now gotten pretty loud, I approached the woman and asked if she needed some help. Concluding her phone call, she told me that she had just been told that her younger brother had been killed in a car accident. I talked with her for a moment or two, and as the gate agent made the final boarding announcement, asked if she still intended to board her flight to Chicago. She said, "No. Right now, I don't even remember why I was going."

The gate agent in this instance was announcing, not communicating. In reality, his job isn't so much to communicate with people as to get them to board an aircraft. But this incident serves as a good example of the fact that if our intention really is to communicate with someone, we should verify that they are in "receiving mode" before uploading our message.

Medical professionals—doctors, nurses, and clinicians of all flavors—are called upon to deliver news, some of it quite painful and difficult. In October 2006, ABC's *Nightline* did a show on "Delivering Bad News to Patients" as part of its "Prescriptions for Change" series. One of the persons interviewed on the show was Rhonda Fishel, MD, surgeon and associate chief of surgery at Baltimore's Sinai Hospital. Dealing with a subject that many physicians (and managers) struggle with due to arrogance, overwork, or perhaps a misperception of their role, Dr. Fishel has made it part of her life's work to become a thought leader on the subject of "delivering bad news well."

> *If our intention really is to communicate with someone, we should verify that they are in "receiving mode" before uploading our message.*

In her interview with *Nightline*, Dr. Fishel underscored the importance of explaining information to people in terms they understand, and in an appropriate setting. Sit down with them and "give the beeper to someone else," she opined. She also urged that people not be given more news in one session than they can handle. Though couched in a medical setting, her advice is as good for the practicing manager as the practicing physician.[2]

3. **Tell them in a timely manner.** If someone has to break stride and wait for information, it slows them down, and annoys them. One of the biggest (and most preventable) things that infuriates air travelers is the propensity on the part of commercial air carriers to keep passengers in the dark during flight delays. We all know that weather gets bad at times, and that machines occasionally break. The thing we can't abide, however, is having facts withheld or being lied to.

4. **Tell them reliably.** Leaders who get discretionary effort out of people are better informed than others. Make it a point to go and get the information, stay informed, and clarify what you hear, read, or see, so that you've got it right. Strive to make meaning for the benefit of every individual

on the team. It's much better to be informed firsthand than to guess or make it up. With all due respect to the corporate communications gurus, people put a lot more credence in what their immediate leader says over what they read or hear from corporate. Use stories and analogies to help make your point and check frequently for understanding.

5. **Tell them in the mode they want to hear it.** Communication that inspires Oomph! is less formal, less bureaucratic, more frequent, more personal, and more relevant. As leaders, we must understand the fact that people process and absorb information differently. If we are truly to make meaning, we must respect and adjust to those differences. As a case in point, it has been said that successfully communicating with Generation Y members means using a medium that is compatible with whatever electronic device they happen to have in their hands at the moment. That may be something the rest of us just have to get used to.

6. **Unfreeze the gears.** One thing that a career in leadership has taught me is that people don't process information very well when they are scared, tired, or consumed by other things. Hence, it is important for us as leaders to be mindful of what shape our folks are in—"where their heads are at," to put it crudely. It is often necessary to intervene in some way.

Shortly after my arrival in the ER, the place got slammed by an onslaught of arriving ambulances and one medevac chopper. After each bout of frenetic activity, someone would crank up a boombox and play a couple cuts of a staff member's favorite music. It clearly worked for them, and although it was keeping me awake, the realization of what was going on caused me to conclude that I had come to the right place.

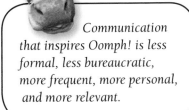

Communication that inspires Oomph! is less formal, less bureaucratic, more frequent, more personal, and more relevant.

Similarly, I watched (on A&E Television) the riveting story of Sir Ernest Shackleton's ill-fated but incredible attempt at the first overland crossing of the Antarctic continent in 1914. Shackleton's work was never-ending, dangerous, and pressure-laden. I came away with a leadership lesson that seems both appropriate and useful to the modern-day manager.

In the face of enormous adversity (having his ship crushed by the pack ice 350 miles from land, running out of food and fresh water, etc.), Sir Ernest, while attending to one crisis after another, found ways for his crew to enjoy regular moments of levity or celebration even as things were going to hell around them. His theory: that a team consumed by the weight of the burden they were expected to carry couldn't possibly perform at peak level. Shackleton was right.

7. **Listen.** Most of us could stand to do a better job of listening—*really* listening . . . not just to data from a heart monitor, blood test, or e-mail, but to the real pulsating human being who sent that message. We should be listening intently to what the individual is saying, what they are trying to say, and what they are not saying.

I caught myself ignoring this axiom a while back, while visiting my mom who was confined in a nursing home. While she tried mightily to tell me something, repeatedly jabbing one of her wizened fingers toward the floor, I ignored her, confident that her Alzheimer's-induced muttering was completely pointless. Then, I happened to look down and notice that one of my shoelaces was untied, something she has been protecting me from for fifty years. My six-foot frame suddenly shrunk about four feet.

Most of us could stand to do a better job of listening—really listening.

Folks, if we do that to our young children and our elderly parents—and we do—we sure as hell do it to our employees, patients/customers, and colleagues.

Promise me—no, promise yourself—that you will vacate your office for a half-hour this week, no matter what your workload is, and go ask your people what kinds of things keep them from doing their very best work. Ask them for a solution, hear them out, and give them an "up" or "down" decision on the spot—no waffling! Regardless of that decision, unless there is one heck of a good reason not to, grant them the authority right then and there to fix the matter. My bet is you'll be so pleasantly surprised by the results you will soon look forward to doing this every week.

Promise yourself that you will vacate your office for a half-hour this week . . . and go ask your people what kinds of things keep them from doing their very best work.

CHAPTER SUMMARY

1. Leaders are not communicating unless they are making meaning.
2. People have basic information needs that must be met as a condition of being competent and reasonably well-directed.
3. Communicate *with* people, not *at* them.
4. Leaders who get discretionary effort out of people are better informed than others. They realize it's better to be informed firsthand than to guess or make it up.
5. People put a lot more credence in what their immediate leader says over what they read from corporate.
6. The communication pattern of leaders who get good discretionary effort tends to be less formal, less bureaucratic, more frequent, more personal, and more relevant.
7. We should listen to what people are saying, what they are trying to say, and what they are not saying.

MONDAY MORNING, 8AM

1. Before you say a word to anyone (other than "good morning"), go on a thirty-minute listening tour. Take note of what you're hearing, its tone, context, etc., and also what you're not hearing (laughter?).

2. Look for ways you can "turn down the volume" so you have a better chance of being heard, and so your message can be separated from the din and appreciated.

It's cancer . . . I don't know why you're upset. You're small-chested anyway. —Physician to patient[3]

19

THE CUSTOMER CONNECTION

To my customer.
I may not have the answer, but I'll find it.
I may not have the time, but I'll make it.
—Unknown

In a presentation to a group of high-end resort operators, I remarked that, were I in their shoes, I would be terrified by the dwindling prospects of being able to deliver good service. My rationale was (and is) that it's nigh unto impossible to deliver something you've never seen or experienced, and that is exactly where the majority of their twenty-something-year-old employees find themselves. It's not their fault. That's just the way it is.

Few would argue that the state of personally delivered customer service in the U.S. is at an all-time low. That's one reason millions of us have taken to buying lots of what we buy on the Internet. And while e-tail shopping is hardly flawless, two of its greatest attractions are the absence of clueless or surly service reps, and avoidance of the long waits that inspired Wallace Wilkins's book *Please Hold: 102 Things To Do While You Wait on the Phone.*

Yep, there's an awful lot of bad customer service out there. But it's not due to a shortage of books and seminars to teach the unenlightened how to be nice to people trying desperately to give them their money. And it's not because customer service employees are innately rude. OK, some are, but most aren't. Where service is lousy, it's often because we as managers haven't equipped our employees to provide the good service that we'd like to believe differentiates us.

It is perhaps obvious that the best route to happy customers is happy employees. That's not a 100 percent direct relationship—oh, that it were that simple. But it is patently clear that you can hardly have happy customers with disgruntled employees serving them. Just ask most air travelers. And yet our message is not—repeat, *not*—about creating an atmosphere of bliss, where your employees are so thrilled with their pay, benefits, and working conditions that they can't help but delight your customers. No, much of what creates a great workplace is whether or not your internal systems allow (and require) people to do their best work . . . work they can be proud of.

The nature of organizations is such that there is often a substantial disconnect between those who make corporate policy and those who are tasked with delivering customer service. One thing that those of us charged with making policy would do well to keep in mind is that good employees won't suffer dumb processes.

In an important study released in 2006, Towers Perrin identified the following five top drivers of employee engagement (engagement being loosely defined as the likelihood of the individual remaining with the organization, together with their willingness to contribute discretionary effort):

1. Having the opportunity to learn and develop skills.
2. Having recently (within the last year) improved their skills and capabilities.
3. The organization's reputation as an employer.
4. Having input to the decision-making process.
5. The organization's focus on customer satisfaction.[1]

Though the first four of the above "engagement drivers" are fairly obvious, the extent to which an organization is seriously committed to maintaining positive customer relationships is perhaps the "sleeper" on the list. We just don't often think about employee connectedness to the organization hinging on how the customer is treated. Yet it is, and how!

As has already been well-established, people truly want to take pride in their work. Good chefs will tell you, for example, that they get absolutely pumped by preparing great meals and watching appreciative guests devour the food. The premise works the same way in reverse, but with added impact. If a chef has to make do with third-rate meats purchased by a cheap or ignorant corporate buyer, he or she isn't going to be able to deliver great meals. People not only are dispirited by being involved in distributing schlock goods or services, they also are personally embarrassed by it! No one wants to be embarrassed.

SCHLOCH STUFF

I will long remember a conversation with a seatmate on a flight from Minneapolis to Atlanta. The fellow was the general counsel of a firm that manufactures electrical products, based in the Twin Cities, Minnesota, area. He was extremely bright and offered up some helpful hints on the editing of this book. What struck me, though, was that, in telling me about what he did, he introduced (without naming) his company by saying, "We manufacture and distribute some really sh*tty electrical products." His embarrassment in being associated with the firm's products was palpable. He went on to tell me about the myriad social and political activities he was engaged in outside of work, and it became readily apparent where his discretionary effort was (and wasn't) going. Like the chef with the poor-quality meat above, this executive could not summon up much Oomph! for the products his company manufactured.

> *People not only are dispirited by being involved in distributing schlock goods or services, they are personally embarrassed by it!*

HOOH ME UP

When my cable Internet service quit working, I told the service rep on the phone that I suspected the cable modem as the culprit. Having experienced frequent service outages, I felt pretty confident about my diagnosis. I told the call center rep that no technician need come out *without* a replacement modem. Impossible, she said, due to company policy. I pressed the point. Of course, the guy showed up . . . modemless. He determined, as had I, that the problem was as simple as a burned-out modem, grumbled something unkind about his company's stupid rules, and returned the next day with a working modem. Wasted were his time, my time, and the company's money and service reputation. Like the attorney for the electrical products company, it is extremely doubtful that this guy spends much of his discretionary capacity on the job.

Extra Miler: Kervin Sweet, Chick-fil-A—"Good morning! Welcome to the best Chick-fil-A in Florida!" booms the commanding voice of Kervin Sweet, a dining room host at the quick-service chain's restaurant on Jacksonville's busy Southside Boulevard. After working for nearly thirty years in his family's funeral business, Kervin embarked on a second career when store owner/

operator Jeromy Williams hired him, impressed by Kervin's zeal for life and enthusiasm—a genuine enthusiasm that comes from the heart of a man who spent years dealing with grieving families.

Chick-fil-A, has, for a number of years now, employed people in the position of dining room host, to clean up, bus tables when necessary, and take care of guest needs, consistent with the company's Second Mile Service standard. When was the last time you saw that under the golden arches?

What makes Kervin stand out, even among his Chick-fil-A colleagues, is his intuition and ability to anticipate customers' needs even before they're expressed. "He has a good eye," says Jeromy. "He can tell by the look on somebody's face if they've forgotten something at the counter, or if their order isn't quite right. And he jumps right on it every time. Our customers love him. They really do. When he's not here, they'll ask, 'Where's Kervin? I thought he usually worked this time of day.'"

A recent extended illness kept Kervin out of work for several weeks, prompting many customers to ask if Kervin was OK, or if he still worked there. What we see with Kervin illuminates several of Chick-fil-A's processes—processes that work to the benefit of the company's customers, employees, and bottom line:

1. The hiring process gives store operators and managers great autonomy to staff their businesses with those "great ingredients" we talked about in chapter 12, even when a candidate's experience falls outside that of other, more "traditional" quick-service restaurant workers. Jeromy recognized in Kervin a quality that he knew would serve his business well, and he put it to optimum use.

2. Second Mile Service at Chick-fil-A is a process itself. It's not just that the standard is excellent customer service; it's a clearly defined set of behaviors identified by a clearly understood moniker. Every team member at Chick-fil-A knows the term Second Mile Service, and knows what it means.

3. The company has done a great job of systematizing the gathering and delivery of feedback—both positive and corrective—to store operators, managers, and team members.

Here are some examples of Kervin-related comments either written on customer comment cards or submitted online through the company's website (www.chick-fil-a.com):

This doesn't even feel like a fast-food restaurant. I mean, the service is fast, but with Kervin, and the folks behind the counter, you just don't get that fast-food feeling.

"Kervin was awesome! This is the first time I've ever felt like leaving a tip in a fast-food restaurant!"

I had lunch yesterday (7/19/06) at the Southside Blvd. (Tinseltown) Chick-fil-A. No sooner did I walk in the door than the employee behind the counter greeted me in what must be the friendliest and most welcoming manner I have ever encountered. If I recall correctly, his name was Kervin; he was an older African-American gentleman. He made me feel almost as if I were a visitor in his home, rather than a customer at a fast-food restaurant. This employee most definitely deserves to be commended in the highest manner possible, and should be held as a shining example of how to treat every customer.

Kervin was awesome! This is the first time I've ever felt like leaving a tip in a fast-food restaurant!

Kervin Sweet goes the second mile, not just in his welcoming manner, but in deed as well. Suppose a mother walks in, with one child on her hip and the other held by the hand. Kervin will go up to the woman and say, "Ma'am, why don't you have a seat? What would you and your children like today? I'll go up and order it for you, and bring it out when it's ready. You just take a load off your feet and get settled here. You're gonna be glad you came to see us today!"

Suppose someone drops a drinking straw. Almost before the straw hits the floor, Kervin has replaced it and offered the customer a refill. I expect that when I'm paying thirty-plus bucks for my meal, but not when the bill comes in under $5.

"Another thing about Kervin," Jeromy tells us, "he never complains. He finds joy in everything he does, whether it's taking out the trash, visiting with a customer, cleaning equipment, changing the peanut oil, or helping a family whose child has spilled a drink."

Jeromy holds Kervin up as an example—the personification of Chick-fil-A's Second Mile Service. In orientation, he tells people, "Kervin would be a good role model to follow. But you'll have to go above and beyond to keep up with him."

CALL CENTER INSANITY

Organizations that get the benefit of Oomph! take deliberate, preemptive steps to avoid putting their workers in the line of fire of angry customers. By definition, this includes taking action to minimize the likelihood of having angry customers in the first place. Anyone who has ever waited in line to be seated in a half-empty restaurant with only two servers on duty or at a retail checkout where every other lane is closed knows how this comes to pass.

As suggested by the Towers Perrin engagement study, people who know that the organization is committed to satisfying customers are much more likely to put everything they've got into serving their customers. Those who believe otherwise will not.[2]

Nowhere is this principle violated more frequently or more egregiously than in the realm of customer service call centers. Let's just call them call centers because, as we all know, there isn't a lot of "customer service" going on.

If your company has a call center, the first thing you *must* do is to cut the hold time. Whatever it takes. Just do it. Beyond the obvious damage this does to customer service, it's just the start of a vicious cycle. You make your customers wait. They get understandably irate. When the call is finally answered, they take it out on the service rep who isn't responsible for the problem instead of the executive who is. The rep is demoralized and doesn't provide good service.

Organizations that get the benefit of Oomph! take deliberate, preemptive steps to avoid putting their workers in the line of fire of angry customers.

I've always wondered if there might be a connection between customer hold time and employee satisfaction, so I performed a quick, unscientific test. I called the regular reservation lines of four major airlines: Southwest and Continental, which both have above-average employee satisfaction reputations, even in the post-9/11 era, and US Airways and American, whose employee *dis*satisfaction has received a lot of press. There was no wait at all for Southwest, and Continental's hold time was just under two minutes. US Airways told me my call was important to them for five minutes and sixteen seconds before answering, and after seven minutes, I hung up on American. I didn't have Dr. Wilkins's book, and ran out of things to do.

A couple of years ago, our primary-care physician moved away and we had to pick another doctor. Our insurance carrier (and probably yours) requires customers to notify them when they change their primary-care physician, and so I called the company one afternoon to register the change, steeling myself for what I knew would likely be a frustrating, if not infuriating, experience. I was not disappointed.

What follows is a direct, verbatim transcript of the call. It's not an exaggeration for comic effect. This is *exactly* what happened.

[Ring]

Thank you for calling [company name withheld]. So that we can best serve you, your call may be recorded for quality purposes. While our customer service associates are dedicated to assisting you, the written terms of your contract will prevail. [In other words, if the person you talk to happens to be helpful, don't hold us to it.] *Please have your member or contract number ready.*

[Pause]

Welcome to customer service. If you are a customer or member, press 1. [I pressed 1]

Please enter the numeric portion of the member or contract number, followed by the pound sign. [Fair enough, but why do I think they're going to ask me this same question again? I entered my member number.]

You entered [my member number.] If this is correct, press 1. [I pressed 1]

Please hold while we transfer you to the team that services your account.

[Long pause. Ring]

Please select from the following six options. [Six options?! Where's my "team"? Let me get a pen to write this down!]

If you are calling in regards to eligibility, prescription benefits or participating pharmacies, emergency services, primary-care physician, co-payment, or a general overview, press 1. [I guess that was the first of the six options.]

If you are calling to request an address change . . ..

[I pressed 1. I heard something in there about primary-care physician.]

Please enter the numeric portion of the member or contract number, followed by the pound sign. [I knew it! I entered my member number . . . again.]

The member or contract number is [my member number.] If this is correct, press 1. [I pressed 1. Are you still with me?]

Please hold.

[Pause]

Welcome to the eligibility and benefits menu. For co-payment information, press 1. For information regarding prescription benefits, press 2. For general information, press 3. [I pressed 3.]

Welcome to the general information menu. For a general overview of your benefits, press 1. For information regarding emergency services, press 2. For information regarding your primary-care physician, press 3. [Eureka! I pressed 3.]

We're sorry, we cannot process your request at this time.

On its face, this sounds like an example of bad customer service. And, of course, it is. But more than that, it demonstrates one of the things that turns Oomph! off.

As you might imagine, I did persist, and eventually I reached a human, somewhere in the United States. She was well-trained, pleasant enough, and, while I would hardly say she was "dedicated to assisting me," she wasn't overtly opposed to doing so. When I finally got her on the line, the first words out of her mouth were, "Thank you for calling [company name withheld]. How can I provide you with excellent customer service today?"

"I'm sorry," I said, "I appreciate your asking. But you've missed your chance."

Only because I had prepared myself mentally for the insanity I knew I would encounter was I able to be civil to the woman on the other end of the line. After all, she wasn't responsible for the idiot system I had just encountered. I told her why I had called, and she handled my request quickly, efficiently, and accurately.

But when I asked her if she had any idea of the nonsense I had to go through to get her on the line, she spoke as though she fully expected my question. And although she didn't say so, I suspected that just about every person she talked to that day, and every day, complained about the "system."

Every day, she and her co-workers must listen to and acknowledge the frustrations of customers—frustrations that the organization deliberately and systemically inflicts on those customers just moments before they get to speak with her. She can't possibly put all her discretionary effort into her work. Why the hell would she even want to?

There are no traffic jams along the extra mile. —Roger Staubach

CHAPTER SUMMARY

1. The best route to happy customers is happy employees.
2. Organizations that get the benefit of Oomph! take deliberate, preemptive steps to avoid putting their workers in the line of fire of angry customers.
3. The quality of an organization's reputation with customers (for service or product excellence) has everything to do with employee connectedness to the organization, and the willingness to part with discretionary effort.

MONDAY MORNING, 8AM

1. In as unobtrusive a manner as possible, arrange to spend an hour this week observing front-line employees interacting with customers. Are they pumped? Are they prideful, or are there some aspects of the customer interface system that are sucking the life out of them?

2. Take twenty minutes and take stock of the opportunities that your employees have to let you and the organization know about aspects of the customer interface systems that prevent them from doing their very best work. Be honest.

SECTION SIX

OOMPH! RULES

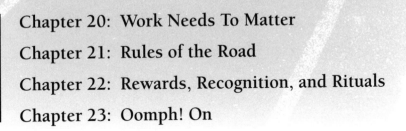

WORK NEEDS TO MATTER

*The more I want to get something done, the
less I call it work.* —Richard Bach

One factor that, more than almost any other, stimulates the exertion of discretionary effort—and whose absence stifles it—is the knowledge that one's work is important, that it makes a difference. People need to know not only that their work makes a difference in the organization, but at least, to some degree, that it makes a difference in the world. They need to know that whatever place their work holds in the grand scheme of things, be it great or small, that it *really* makes a difference that what they do . . . they do well.

In certain jobs and professions, people know, without any outside reinforcement, that their work matters. Others might need to be taught this important concept, or at least reminded of it, at regular intervals.

I have a friend who is a gynecological oncologist. He treats—and is often instrumental in saving the lives of —women with deadly cancers. He goes to bed every night knowing, without any doubt, that what he does matters and that it's vital that he do it very, very well. Notwithstanding the fact that he's paid well for his services, this guy (a married father of five, who's very involved in his community, and has lots on his plate), pours copious amounts of discretionary effort into his work. He has constant reminders that his work matters.

Now, let's consider someone who works in the bowels of a large government bureaucracy. She gets precious little recognition or positive reinforcement in her work, and she never gets the message that what she does is important. She rarely, if ever, comes face-to-face with a paying customer (known in her world as a taxpayer), and she never sees the fruits of her labor, except twice a month when a sum of money is deposited electronically into her checking account.

How does she manage to scrape up even one ounce of discretionary effort? Without disparaging all government workers, the sad truth is that she probably doesn't. But she could.

The world is populated largely by people who come to work every day, in for-profit enterprises, do an adequate job, and wait out retirement or a better deal, perhaps because they lack an abiding sense that what they do matters to anyone else on the planet.

You don't need to work in the public sector to experience the doldrums that accompany a lack of understanding that your work is important. The world is populated largely by people who come to work every day, in for-profit enterprises, do an adequate job, and wait out retirement or a better deal, perhaps because they lack an abiding sense that what they do matters to anyone else on the planet.

That, or for reasons that are personal, the fire has simply gone out. I witnessed this on a large scale about ten years after leaving FedEx. The company had changed dramatically, becoming much more of a haven for bureaucrats than entrepreneurs, but many of the folks I had worked alongside in the high-growth years opted to stick around, despite the unmistakable feeling that their creativity, ideas, and decisions weren't as welcome as they once had been. Some stayed and thrived. Many did not. You could see it on their faces and in their gait, and hear it in their voices. Yet most chose not to leave, even though they were clearly less than enthused. Truth be known, many were just mailing it in, probably afraid to make a move. Sadly, with few exceptions, no one had the heart to show them the door. Perhaps they should have. If people have "unplugged," either plug them back in, or help them find another receptacle.

24 Hour Fitness. We asked a group of workers for 24 Hour Fitness what makes them work and, in many cases, work harder than they have to, putting so much of themselves into what they do. One woman's comments pretty much summed up the consensus of the group when she said, "We get excited about Sally losing fifty pounds. That's what we're working for—for Sally to lose that fifty pounds, feel better, control her diabetes, get a date!"

Extra Miler: Lorrie Green, Baptist Medical Center—Lorrie Green serves as an ambassador in the emergency department (ED) at Baptist Medical Center in Jacksonville, Florida. Lorrie's job is to serve the non-clinical needs of patients and their families during their visits to Baptist's ED. That means, among other things, checking on patients and families, and updating them on the status of the patient's visit ("You're next. . . . Someone will be here in five minutes to take you to X-ray. . . . I'm so sorry. We're backed up with a bad car accident. It's probably going to be another hour before the doctor can see you, etc."). She helps make patients and their families more comfortable and takes some of the edge off what is rarely a pleasant experience. We think it's a splendid idea, and one that more EDs should adopt. The following letter, from a couple who found themselves unexpectedly under Lorrie's care, is typical of the feedback she receives from her customers.

We get excited about Sally losing fifty pounds. That's what we're working for—for Sally to lose that fifty pounds, feel better, control her diabetes, get a date!

Dear Lorrie,

We cannot tell you how much we appreciate the manner in which you helped us get through our stay in the emergency room tonight. We know that what you did for us, and for me in particular, was your job. But the way you did it was extremely comforting and made us feel much more at ease. You made a bad situation tolerable. You do your job well, and truthfully, you're worth your weight in gold. We're not surprised that you're on three committees. Actually, we wouldn't be surprised if they had you running the entire hospital someday. It was our good fortune to have met you today.

Thanks again for all your help. It really meant a lot to us.

While traveling in their recreational vehicle through northern Florida on their way from New York, the man whose wife wrote the above letter fell and sustained an injury that required emergency attention. She pulled the

RV over to the side of Interstate 95, near downtown Jacksonville, and called 911. The ambulance arrived and took the two to Baptist's ED.

The wife was understandably upset. Her husband was hurt, they were in an unfamiliar city, and they didn't know a soul in town. Adding to the couple's anxiety was the fact that their expensive, thirty-three-foot RV was parked unattended on the side of a very busy eight-lane expressway.

Lorrie summoned a cab and helped the driver discern, based on the woman's description, exactly where they might find the RV. With the wife back on the road in her home-on-wheels, Lorrie "talked her in" through the confusing side streets from the highway to the hospital, and, in perhaps the most magnanimous gesture of all, helped her find parking, always at a premium at a hospital, for a vehicle that took up six spaces. While Lorrie sees that as just part of her job, it's clear that the couple recognized it as going the extra mile.

SEEING HOW YOUR WORK MATTERS TO THE CUSTOMER

Think about your workforce. Do you have anyone who, in the natural course of things, never comes in contact with a real-live, paying customer? If you're like most managers in most organizations, the answer is yes. Most organizations have legions of these behind-the-scenes folks pulling on oars in the galley, while the captain and deckhands do their work in full view of the public.

Pick just about any business: For every person in front of the customer, there are people behind the scenes who make things tick. Without them, there would be no salespeople, and no sales. No delivery truck drivers, and no deliveries. No cashiers. And no cash.

And yet, absent intentional and strategically oriented measures to combat the problem, most of these people will never see, hear, or smell a real, paying customer in the course of doing their work. Ultimately, for most of us, it comes down to the degree to which we can relate our work to the value derived by the end customer.

To be sure, in the American workforce, there are more people whose job it is to serve internal customers than there are those who serve external ones. Many people are able to find intrinsic value in serving the internal customer. But without managers clearly making the end-customer connection, a person can't possibly realize the full potential that's out there for how their work matters. People often lose sight of the very important notion that their work has consequence. As leaders, we need to remind them. That may mean that we need to manufacture opportunities for them to have a real customer experience.

> *People often lose sight of the very important notion that their work has consequence. As leaders, we need to remind them.*

One of the banks with which we do business has done exactly that. Every bank employee, including the guy who pushes the broom around, is assigned to a customer account. They are expected to talk with the customer at least twice a year (by phone or in person), take them to lunch on their birthday, and, if the customer has a problem, to get it solved. Granted, bank management is judicious in making these customer assignments (the janitor is not assigned to a $10 million trust account), but people *do* take it seriously and get to feel the weight of having an obligation to a real, paying customer. Moreover, it serves as a frequent reminder to them of what the organization is in business for, and where their paycheck comes from.

> *I like this life. I don't know if I can say why. I don't know if I have the right words. I'm proud of the fact that I got into it and succeeded at it. Buffalo are an important part in American history. There's the pride and prestige in raising them. The meat is better. Our working corral is the best in the world. Nobody disputes that.* —Ray O. Smith, buffalo rancher[1]

A number of years ago I was working on a consulting assignment for a company that made hospital products—specifically, tubing assemblies used in hospitals to deliver intravenous medication, fluids, and nutrition to patients. The charge to our consulting team was to investigate the plant's high employee turnover and quality problems, and fix them.

I was surprised to see how labor-dependent this very manual operation was. These people made their product through a tedious process: dipping the ends of plastic tubing into a solvent to make the ends sticky, then attaching joints, couplings, valves, and other apparatus to them, in order to make the completed assembly. Each person was expected to complete hundreds of these assemblies a day, going through monotonous, repetitive motions that today have been replaced by robotics. You're falling asleep just reading about their work. Imagine *doing it.* Day in and day out.

It was no wonder that people were falling asleep on the job (literally), and that their error and burnout rates were high. There were vacancies in the department, and turnover was nearing 100 percent per year, despite offering the best compensation and benefits package of any employer in the region (which helps explain why you get whacked for more than $80 for one of these tubes, and the attached bag, in the hospital.)

We MBA-types came in and began recommending all the things we had learned in business school, things like job enhancement and job variety. All with little effect.

Then, one of the more experienced guys on the consulting team suggested the following: Put everyone in the department on a bus, and take them down to the regional hospital nineteen miles from the plant. There they can see these tubing assemblies they make all day long doing their work. Let's see if that makes a difference.

So we rented a yellow school bus, loaded up all the manufacturing employees in the department, and drove to the hospital for a firsthand look. I had not anticipated the excitement and enthusiasm that I saw from these heretofore ughing factory workers, as they witnessed the very tubes their hands had wrought being used to deliver lifesaving medication and nourishment to patients.

The mother of a young girl who had been badly burned in an automobile accident told the group that her daughter had been in such pain after her burns that she talked only of wanting to die, until the doctor had prescribed a drip of pain medication that allowed her to tolerate the healing process.

When the workers got back from the four-hour trip, they all remarked, "So *that's* what we do. Now we see why we come to work each day." Within weeks, morale rose markedly, as did quality. Turnover dropped, and people began to work with an energy the plant manager hadn't seen since he had arrived six years before. The program was so successful that the plant manager decided to get everyone—not just the assembly workers—in on the deal. Arrangements were made with the hospital to conduct similar tours for the office staff and even the maintenance crew, so that they could see firsthand the connection of their daily work to something that *really* matters, proving that you don't have to be a gynecological oncologist to derive pleasure from saving lives.

A few years ago, I experienced a similar result while doing some leadership training at Pfizer's central research facility in Groton, Connecticut. Introducing myself to each participant group, I mentioned that I found our work with their organization personally rewarding owing to the fact that one of their drugs, Aricept, has extended the useful life of thousands of Alzheimer's patients, one of whom happened to be my mother.

People give their all—their Oomph!— if they think it's important. If they don't, they don't.

One morning during the break, one of the participants, a thirty-something-year-old research scientist, pulled me aside to let me know how much it meant to him hearing about my mom's experience with Aricept. After proudly telling me that he had done some bench work on the compound, he added that this was the first time he had ever heard, or seen, a firsthand account of the results of his work. The moment was truly special for both of us. People give their all—their Oomph!—if they think it's important. If they don't, they don't.

CHICK-FIL-A GRAND OPENINGS ARE A BIG DEAL

In chapter 1, we recounted our visit with Chick-fil-A's Dan Cathy, as he hopped from market to market to open new locations of his family's quick-service chicken restaurants. We were astonished to learn how involved a Chick-fil-A Grand Opening is. It's a big deal.

In preparation for the opening of a new store, experienced team members—the Grand Opening Team, or GOT—are brought in from other locations for a couple of weeks, to train the new staff and get the store customer-ready. Then, one evening in the handful of days before the store opens, the GOT serves dinner at the new location for all new employees and their families, who have a chance to see Second Mile Service done just right, from the beginning.

A few days later comes the next event in the grand opening sequence, Dan's Second Mile Service training, which we referred to in chapter 1. That's right. The president of the $2 billion corporation goes to each grand opening and conducts a customer service training class for the new team members.

As an aside, we've long been of the belief that *who* conducts certain training is almost as important as what's being taught. When Kevin Krolczyk, presi-

203

dent of Dalbec Roofing Company in Long Lake, Minnesota, does the monthly safety training, it's hard for his people to miss the message that safety is one of their top priorities. In the same way, when Bud Mingledorff, CEO of HVAC distributor Mingledorff's, conducts sexual harassment training, there can be no mistake that the company takes its zero-tolerance policy seriously.

Upon the conclusion of Second Mile Service training, all the new employees sit down to a dedication dinner, held at an offsite facility, where the company's mission, purpose, and values are not only explained, but demonstrated, for all new employees to see. In Des Moines, we dined "under the stars" inside the Science Center's planetarium; in Sacramento, the dedication dinner was held in one of the special function rooms at Arco Arena, where everyone was later treated to an NBA game between Sacramento's Kings and the San Antonio Spurs.

All of these events lead up to what has become a signature of a Chick-fil-A opening, the "First One Hundred Customers" celebration held the night before (and into the morning of) the store's opening. Chick-fil-A has developed such stalwart fans over the years that, in advance of each opening, people sign up to be among the store's first customers. The first one hundred to get their names on the list camp out overnight in the parking lot of the restaurant, often with Dan, who wears Chick-fil-A pajamas festooned with the chain's now-famous "Eat Mor Chikin" cows (a mascot near and dear to our hearts). Their reward is a book of coupons entitling them to free Chick-fil-A food for a year!

Many people, ourselves included, have wondered why the company president makes it his duty to officiate at every store's grand opening, as Dan does. The answer is simple. Chick-fil-A makes a big deal of every grand opening, because every grand opening is a big deal! It's all to convey one message—a message the company's leaders don't believe can be conveyed as effectively any other way. And that message is: "What you do here is important. It matters. It's a big deal. And it's important to us that we do this better than any of our competitors."

When they have a family dinner, served by pros, when the company president makes it a point to personally deliver customer service training, then treats the team to a nice offsite dedication dinner with something special planned, then camps out, rain or shine, in the parking lot, getting three hours' sleep—four max—before serving chicken biscuits to one hundred equally bleary-eyed raving fans, the people (many of them teenagers) starting their jobs in a Chick-fil-A restaurant can't help but get the distinct impression that *what they do matters*. And it matters a lot. It's not just serving chicken sandwiches and waffle fries.

CHAPTER SUMMARY

1. If a person feels that their job is nonessential, they can't help but conclude the same about their level of effort.
2. Some jobs (surgeon, firefighter) lend themselves more naturally to understanding why one's work matters. It is our job, as leaders, to make sure everyone makes the connection, always—no exceptions or excuses.
3. If people have "unplugged," either plug them back in, or help them find another receptacle.
4. Note to senior leaders—Don't tell your people why their work matters, show them.

MONDAY MORNING, 8AM

1. Take an inventory of every position in your organization and answer the question, "How can I be sure people doing this job KNOW why and how their work (and their effort) matters?"

2. Consider ways that you—like Dan Cathy of Chick-fil-A and Bud Mingledorff of Mingledorff's—can adjust your own priorities in order to vividly demonstrate to your people what matters most.

CHAPTER 21

RULES OF THE ROAD

*You don't want to just be great. . . . You want to be known as
the ONLY ones who do what you do.* —Jerry Garcia

Most of us eventually come to understand that—just as we have to pay the price of a lottery ticket if we hope to win—winning at work comes with a price, too. We have to acquire knowledge, tools, and license to perform our particular craft. We have to practice. One of the prices paid by every winning organization is the imposition of some rules and standards. It is impossible to have a well-functioning enterprise running at a high rate of speed if everybody is making it all up on the fly, and deciding on their own how the place will be run.

The key for leaders who want to see Oomph! is distinguishing between rules that enable people to do their best work and those that grind people down to a dysfunctional nub.

RULES ARE MADE TO BE BROKEN—SOMETIMES

Every organization has (or should have) two kinds of rules or policies: a small set of core maxims that are just plain inviolable, no matter what, and a modestly sized group of policies that are regarded more as customs.

Type 1. The first group is easy. It should contain the very few cardinal rules that govern the organization—generally things that pertain to the minimum standards of human behavior: ethics, integrity, and the like. They apply to everybody, they are not subject to varying interpretations, and both the letter and spirit are unmistakable. If you've got more than a half-dozen of these, you're either in a really weird business, you're hiring the wrong kind of people, or you've got a bureaucracy run amok.

As easy as this one should be, many organizations struggle with it, especially when it comes to enforcing these rules. We recently became aware of a situation in a Florida location of a publicly owned, casual-themed restaurant company. In order to inflate revenues and achieve their maximum bonus, the store's general manager, aided and abetted by two operating managers, decided to "cook" the restaurant's books in addition to their customers' dinners. Though the general manager was fired, the other two culprits remain on the payroll, even though the organization's policies clearly state that theft and dishonesty will not be tolerated. Hmmm.

Type 2. This set deals with everything else—matters that may sometimes be black-and-white but in other cases are less clear, requiring some judgment and discretion on the part of managers. In the latter case, managers should be encouraged—no, required—to take into account the facts of the issue (including possible mitigating factors), the culture of the organization, and the policy itself . . . and then do what's right.

Unfortunately, as organizations become larger, the quest for operational consistency and the desire to minimize risk that emanates from the exercise of managerial discretion causes many to enact all sorts of the inviolable, Type 1 policies. The thought process seems to be that if we remove the element of judgment—of decision-making—our actions will be not only more consistent, but also better. Though the intentions are good, the outcome seldom is.

In its early days, FedEx had a policy dictating that should a ground vehicle (van, tug, loader, etc.) collide with an aircraft, the employee operating the vehicle would be terminated—period, end of discussion. No manager had the authority to discern on the basis of possible mitigating circumstances. The intent of the policy was pretty clear: The company wanted to send a strong message that—for safety as well as economic reasons—damaging an aircraft was not something that would be taken lightly. Many readers are probably saying to themselves about now, "What's wrong with that?"

Thankfully, at some point, we figured out what *was* wrong with that. A manager in one of our leadership training classes hypothesized, "What if you've got a cargo handler operating a van at night on a poorly lit airport ramp. He is by himself and, as he backs the van up to the aircraft in order to load some last-minute packages, he feels the vehicle bump the aircraft. He gets out of the van, walks around back, and confirms that the two are indeed touching. A visual inspection suggests that there is no damage to either piece of equipment. As he looks around and confirms that there are no witnesses to the event, thoughts go racing through his head about his certain demise if he reports the accident, his need to feed a family, and the like. What does this guy do? What would YOU do?"

Given human nature, an abundance of concern for safety, and a healthy dose of trepidation about some day having to explain to some reporter from *60 Minutes* how a purple and orange airplane fell out of the sky over Chicago and into a crowded schoolyard, the policy was amended to reflect a bit more realism.

MORE IS DEFINITELY NOT BETTER

Next to being on a team captained by a poster child for the "Gross Leadership Failure League," nothing dampens one's willingness to part with discretionary effort more than an overabundance of stupid, inane rules that serve to insult a person's judgment and indeed their status as a competent adult. Anyone who has been employed by a government agency or large corporation is likely familiar with this condition.

By definition, rules serve as a limiter or barrier to the use of independent discretion. They tell the individual or organization that, in this area, we don't want you to do a whole lot of thinking. Rather, do what you're told. Comply.

It seems obvious that, to the degree discretion is limited, so too is the likelihood that discretionary effort will be expended. The more the conscious self is subordinated, the more the individual goes on autopilot, and the more inclined he or she is to "work to the rules." In fact, commercial airline pilots have, for years, used what they term "working to the rules" as an alternative to going on strike. Everything slows down as people simply do what the rules tell them to do—no less, but certainly no more.

While COO at FedEx, Jim Barksdale implemented a practice that made a lot of sense for an organization that was growing more bureaucratic by the day. He put the company's policy manuals on a diet with a simple edict

To the degree discretion is limited, so too is the likelihood that discretionary effort will be expended.

mandating that no new policy could be enacted without two existing ones being sunsetted.

Following are a few acts of preventive maintenance we think will serve your organization well. On the premise that policies are, by definition, things that encourage us to be consistent, we should periodically examine them for fairness, utility, reasonableness, and clarity. Here's a thought: On a regular (at least annual) basis, take a hard look at your policy manual. Whether it's a book, booklet, or just a file of papers shoved in a drawer somewhere, pull that sucker out and examine it. Treat this exercise just like your physician does your annual physical.

1. First thing, put it on your postage scale and weigh it (for real). If we're talking pounds instead of ounces, or if the thing has inexplicably gained weight over the past year, we have the makings of a problem, don't we?

2. Continuing with the physical exam, check the document's cholesterol level. Ask a few people with about an eighth-grade reading comprehension level to read it over, and then check for comprehension. (No, you don't have to actually mention to these folks that they are participating in an idiot-proofing exercise. If you have access to some reasonably with-it eighth-graders, you might solicit their input.) If, like a lot of organizations, you've got lawyers actively involved in drafting or reviewing policy, the thing may more closely resemble a car rental contract than something that is supposed to be a management tool. If what you see doesn't pass the smell test for simplicity, insist that it be rewritten.

3. Next, look at the overall context of the contents. Do they serve to define a few core principles the organization feels strongly about or, instead, virtually shut off managerial thinking? By way of example, I knew it was time to leave my last employer when a senior VP explained to me (with a straight face) that unless a corporate policy expressly indicated that an individual could exercise judgment on a given issue, then their gray matter was to remain dormant. My thoughts turned to the wonderful training film we've mentioned before, *Brain Power*, starring John Houseman, wherein he admonishes managers, "You get paid to think."[1] Thankfully, I soon found the courage to tell "Mr. Empowerment" that my talents henceforth would be used elsewhere.

4. Now, get specific. Look hard, real hard for the stinkers that just don't make sense any-more. Travel/entertainment and compensa-tion/benefit policies and programs are a great place to start. We frequently tell a story about the travel and entertainment policy of one of our clients, which states that *all* meal expenditures must be receipted via an

Look hard, real hard for the stinkers that just don't make sense anymore.

American Express chit in order to be reimbursed. Unless you happen to be an American Express shareholder, think about the sheer lunacy of that little jewel for a moment. My bet is they wind up paying for a lot of steaks when all the person really wanted was a hotdog from a street vendor who didn't accept plastic.

NO A**HOLES RULE

We're sorry (OK, one of us is sorry) that we've been unable to find a more delicate way of making this point.

As we've already established, organizations have all kinds of policies that are ostensibly used to maintain order, discipline, and performance. People get fired (deselected, if you will) for all kinds of reasons every day: for vio-lating a policy, for poor work performance, for not showing up, for showing up late, for stealing, insubordination, using poor judgment—the list goes on and on.

Though we try not to be especially hardnosed and have an intense dislike for bureaucracy, we would propose that most organizations need to adopt one more rule, and indeed one more cause for termination. The rule is that people who demonstrate themselves to be complete (not just occasional) a**holes will be forced to find work elsewhere—preferably with a com-petitor. This condition was originally described by Stanford professor Robert Sutton in an article entitled "More Trouble Than They Are Worth," and in his subsequent book, *The No Asshole Rule.*[2]

You know the kind. If pressed, you could even name a couple in the next ten seconds. We've all met them and, unfortunately, have had way too many days at work spoiled by the one self-centered weasel who thinks he has the market cornered on brains and good ideas, and that everybody is out to get him (they are).

These bozos suck the life out of a workplace and the people in it. Our guess is that customers don't tolerate them any better than do fellow workers. Though we have absolutely no empirical data to back it up, we are utterly convinced that one of the simplest and most effective things you can do in the near term to unleash the discretionary effort in your workplace is to adopt (for real) an unwritten but well-enforced "no a**holes rule."

It is something you should be diligently screening for in the recruiting process. In fact, this is one of the reasons multiple interviews using different raters is a good idea. A well-practiced a**hole with a little bit of savvy can occasionally get by a single hiring manager in the course of a one-hour interview, particularly if that manager is desperate to fill a vacant slot or, heaven forbid, happens to be similarly afflicted. The odds of pulling it off with three people in three separate discussions are remote.

One way you can save a lot of money is by abandoning the ridiculous notion that training, coaching, or transferring someone will somehow mitigate behaviors that are hardwired into the person. The transfer route is, at best, a cruel joke on someone else in the organization. A jerk in accounting will be a jerk in marketing or operations.

Over the course of thousands of hours in the corporate classroom and in scores of executive coaching engagements, we have seen a lot of these folks sent—in a last desperate hope perhaps—to be "fixed." Stop it, now! It won't work. You're wasting your money, giving coaching and training interventions a bad reputation, and blocking others who would benefit from the opportunity.

A jerk in accounting will be a jerk in marketing or operations.

We weren't joking about terminating the employment of these people. You need to stop putting it off, and stop calling it something other than what it is. Take it from a former HR executive who has seen a lot of shaky paper evidence created to justify the demise of someone who simply needed to be told, "I've made a mistake in hiring you, and you in coming to work here. Despite your abilities and qualities, you are never going to be happy, productive, and successful here. Let's do the right thing and let you have a chance to go somewhere else where your talents will be better utilized and appreciated." You don't have to be mean-spirited or nasty about it, but you do have to do it.

CHAPTER SUMMARY

1. You should have two types of policies:
   a. *Type 1.* A few core precepts (ethics, integrity, etc.) ought to be inviolable.
   b. *Type 2.* Most policies should be subject to some interpretation by a thinking manager.
2. When it comes to rules, more is definitely not better.
3. Every organization should adopt an unwritten but well-enforced "no a**holes rule."

MONDAY MORNING, 8am

1. Find someone you are mad at and have them give your policies and employee handbook a thorough "physical," with weigh-in, cholesterol screening, the works.

2. Begin a relentless search for the "FedEx airplane-type policies" that represent a danger to human effort, and perhaps to your business in general.

CHAPTER
22

REWARDS, RECOGNITION, AND RITUALS

We would do this even if we didn't get paid. —Joe Perry, Aerosmith

If you were to spend days and days working feverishly to create the dumbest compensation scheme ever concocted, you simply could not come up with a more ridiculous scheme than the way most of us choose to pay our employees. Think about it: Paying someone according to how long it takes them to do something is a fundamentally bankrupt notion. That has always been the case in "modern" society, but it is especially true in our fast-paced, Internet-age, "I need it now" world. Seriously, do you think it's an accident (or necessity) that lawsuits drag on for years while attorneys shuffle paper back and forth between them?

CLASSICAL MOTIVATION THEORY VS. COWBOY LOGIC

Behavioral theorists (Maslow, Herzberg, Vroom, Adams, Skinner, et al.) are all over the lot in their thinking about if, how, and to what degree, rewards and recognition impact Oomphing and ughing. Indeed, each makes perfectly good arguments about the relative importance of rewards in the motivational scheme of things. Our view, somewhat akin to that of B. F. Skinner, is that people will do what they are incented to do. In a nutshell, those behaviors that lead to positive outcomes (for the individual or team) will be repeated. Those that lead to negative outcomes (or *no* outcome) will generally not be repeated. Simple logic. Cowboy logic.

So, "What's the point?" you ask. Do rewards play a significant role in an individual's decision about how much effort to contribute or not? You bet they do. The correlation certainly isn't lost on us. Really—do you think we took the time to research and write this book just because we felt we had something to share with fellow leaders?

Let's be equally clear, though, in defining what we mean by rewards. We're not just talking about cash (or equivalents) any more than we're limiting the scope to things that are fungible, or tangible. We should be mindful that what represents a reward to one may be a punishment to another. Here again, it's personal.

IT'S PERSONAL

A 2005 poll of 1,002 full-time employees by St. Louis–based Maritz Incentives examined corporate recognition and reward practices relative to employee preferences. The study suggests that we manager-types have a lot to learn about recognition and rewards. It suggests that there is a substantial disparity between how employees are recognized in the workplace and how they actually *want* to be recognized.

According to the study, whether an employee's preferences lean toward non-monetary awards (gift cards, trips, etc.), symbolic awards (trophies, et al.), or something else (cash bonuses), about 80 percent of the time, the individual is not rewarded in the fashion they prefer.

"Managers know the power of positive reinforcement for a job well-done, but this study shows employees are motivated in vastly different ways, and companies still have a long way to go to ensure their employees feel valued," said Mark Peterman, vice president of client solutions at Maritz. He added, "For example, consider public recognition. For some, being honored in front of one's peers is a great award. For others, the thought of being put on display in front of

There is a substantial disparity between how employees are recognized in the workplace and how they actually want *to be recognized.*

their peers embarrasses them. It depends on the culture and preferences of your particular employee base."[1]

The lesson? Based on the premise that people's hearts and minds get captured one at a time, we would do well to apply some twenty-first-century thinking about mass customization to our reward and recognition practices, and reward our folks in the same manner—one at a time.

MASS CUSTOMIZATION AND THE PERSONAL TOUCH

Because of customer relationship management software and the attendant opportunity to create sophisticated databases, most companies have a rich treasure trove of information about their prospects and customers. For two decades, Delta has been my airline of choice. In that time, they have gathered all kinds of information about me, my flying habits, and my preferences.

But, there's a reason I keep going back to Delta, and it has nothing to do with fares, routes, equipment, or frequent flyer programs. Nor does it involve all the information they've got. Rather, consistent perhaps with their southern heritage, many of their people treat me as an individual, rather than "the guy in 2-B." More often than not, when I step off the escalator onto the ticketing level at Memphis International, even at 5:30AM, I am warmly greeted (not just smiled or waved at, but greeted) by name by Verna, Bob, Sam, Brooks, or another of the Delta agents. I'm no rock star, and I'm certainly not alone in getting this treatment. It happens regularly with customers they know. That, folks, is about as warm and personal as it gets in mass commercial air travel these days. We would do well to imbue some of that warmth and personalization into the way we reward and recognize our employees.

Extra Miler: Verna Crutcher, Delta Air Lines—On the Friday after Thanksgiving 2004, I was in the Memphis airport, awaiting a flight. Also waiting in the packed gate area were three soldiers clad in desert combat uniforms headed back to the war in Iraq after a brief R&R visit. As we boarded, a passenger mentioned to the agent handling the boarding process that it would be nice to see those three fellows get a first-class seat, even if he had to contribute his own seat to the deal. The guy behind me muttered a few words of agreement, then, calling to mind Delta's recent near-death experience (bankruptcy), said something about snowballs in hot places.

A few minutes later, each of the soldiers boarded the aircraft, looked at his seat assignment on the boarding card, scanned the seat number markings on the overhead bins, reexamined the boarding pass, shrugged, smiled, and settled into a slightly more comfortable seat for the first leg of a journey back to hell. Soon thereafter, the gate-agent-cum-tooth-fairy, a lady named Verna, boarded the plane, flashed a quick smile, gave the pilots their paperwork, and left.

Owing to a simple act of kindness, at least five people—the three troops, the gate agent, and I—all got our day off to a little nicer start. Some might wonder, "What's the big deal?" The upgrades didn't cost Delta anything, and the gate agent wasn't playing with her own money anyhow. Perhaps in the scheme of things, it wasn't such a big deal. Yet I can recall plenty of less-friendly interactions with airline personnel, and countless evenings standing at airport gates alongside four other guys whose names, like mine, had not yet cleared the upgrade list for two available seats, and all of us secretly wondering who should be shoved in front of that infernal beeping motorized cart to make the odds a little better.

No, the big deal, at least from my perspective, is that such an act was anything but unusual for this lady. Somehow, she manages to show up every day for work at "oh-dark-thirty," spring-loaded to inject a little warmth and decency into what has become a pretty miserable experience. Acts of grace and kindness are, for her, anything but random. They are her habit, her custom.

Got any folks like that in your life, or on your payroll? You know the ones. They seldom make noise, preferring instead to go about their business with quiet efficiency. They are never too busy to hold a door, help a stranger, call or visit when they know someone needs it, or reach for their own billfold when someone less fortunate needs a hand. And lest we forget, these folks don't just make life a little smoother, they are good for business.

Between us, in the last two decades, we have spent in excess of two entire years (24/7) aboard Delta jets. The decision to habitually book on Delta has nothing to do with fares, food, or freebies, but instead, the fact that—for now at least—they seem to have a larger supply of Vernas than their domestic network competitors do.

A long-time Delta customer service agent, Verna has experienced up-close and personal some of the best and—more recently—worst years in the history of commercial passenger aviation. Yet, as we have seen with Dr. Benjamin and Hubert Allen of the Pebble Beach Company, Verna's smile is as genuine as it is ever-present.

One morning in October 2006, as I approached gate A-29 at the Memphis airport, Verna rushed out from behind the counter to greet me, with an even bigger smile than usual. The extra radiance owed to her having just been notified that she was to receive Delta's Chairman's Award, the highest honor bestowed upon any employee at Delta Air Lines. Soon thereafter, at an elaborate function held at the company's Atlanta headquarters, she was formally honored for her many accomplishments. In addition to some nifty gifts, a plaque honoring her was installed near the boarding door of a Delta aircraft, in view of all who enter.

The personal touch Verna gives—out of her own Oomph!—was personally rewarded by Delta, encouraging her to continue to spend her discretionary effort for the betterment of the company and her customers.

DOWN 'N DIRTY

Having Vernas in your life is seldom an accident. Rather, it's something you can actually exert some influence over, by:

1. Consciously recruiting people who are not only competent, but nice. Great cakes start with great ingredients—it's that simple.

2. Making it a point to let special people know that they are special—that you appreciate what they do and will try to help them when and where you can. Here's a little exercise that may help: Make a list of the three most special people (to you) at your workplace. Then, answer the question, "Why does this person stay with me, with this organization?" Our bet is this will lead to a very good conversation.

3. Last, and most important, exhibiting more "Verna-like" behavior of our own. Would it really be all that difficult to resolve that twice a day (once each in the morning and afternoon), you are going to go out of your way to do (or say) something nice for someone else?

RECOGNITION TAKES TIME

The Maritz study prescribes some common-sense steps managers can take to up the gain from their reward and recognition programs. First among them is simply spending time with each employee to find out how they are motivated. What turns them on and off? What are their goals and aspirations?

How do they like to receive rewards, and from whom? Periodically touch base with them to ensure that your efforts are working.[2]

Almost telepathically, we can sense some resistance building up in some readers about now. "Geez, this is going to take a lot of time. I've got a lot of people who report to me, and a lot to get done. I'm not sure I have time for this stuff." Really? So when (never mind how) do you intend to get all that stuff done with a dispirited, disengaged workforce? What will that cost you?

According to the Maritz poll, 60 percent of respondents felt that their company should refresh its recognition efforts with some new and different awards. Ditto for the communications efforts surrounding such programs. Further, we are reminded to ensure that our reward and recognition efforts don't leave out any employee group. Include 'em all, from sales reps to the folks who toil in obscurity on the third shift in facility maintenance. That doesn't mean that everybody *gets* rewards necessarily, just that they are eligible, and that the reward is meaningful to them if and when it comes.

People—all of us—want to know that our effort matters, really matters. We need to be shown how it matters and, more important, we need to see clear and compelling connections between what we do and why the organization is in business. Otherwise, the decline in our effort is at hand.

One of the clearest ways to create that connection is to provide a direct and significant link between an individual's pay and what they produce. Many would have us believe that we must pay people for time, because federal or state wage and hour laws require us to do so—*au contraire*. In a nutshell, as long as you are complying with minimum wage requirements and the updated requirements of the Fair Labor Standards Act that govern the payment of overtime, you can pay people on pretty much any basis you want to.

NUCOR STEEL: PERFORMANCE-BASED COMPENSATION

One of the very few U.S.-based, globally competitive steel companies, Nucor Corporation in Charlotte is the largest steel producer in the United States, with sales and net income of $14.8 billion and $1.8 billion respectively in 2006. According to the company's published data, Nucor is also the nation's largest recycler, having recycled approximately seventeen million tons of scrap steel (largely from autos) in 2004.[3]

With seven thousand non-union employees in an otherwise heavily unionized industry, Nucor squares off against its Pac-Rim competitors by focusing like a laser on building and operating efficient, high-quality steel manufacturing facilities. With an organizational structure as streamlined as its steel mills, the company operates with only about two dozen headquarters staffers (yes, you read that correctly) and four or fewer layers of management. No company jets, no executive dining rooms or company cars, no employment contracts, no frills, no fluff. Everyone has the same benefits plan.

Inspired largely by former CEO F. Kenneth Iverson, the company has clearly repudiated authoritarian management methods and operates with four simple employee relations principles:

1. Management is obligated to manage Nucor in such a way that employees will have the opportunity to earn according to their productivity.
2. Employees should be able to feel confident that if they do their jobs properly, they will have a job tomorrow.
3. Employees have the right to be treated fairly and must believe that they will be.
4. Employees must have an avenue of appeal when they believe they are being treated unfairly.

> *The more we diminish money as our chief goal, the more*
> *passion we can put into our efforts.* —Matt Chambers,
> founder and CEO, Confederate Motor Company[4]

Covering everyone from the mill floor to the corner office, Nucor's incentive plans feature serious upside potential, a pay-at-risk component, and group as well as individual goals.

All employees are covered under one of four basic plans, each featuring incentives related to meeting specific goals and targets:

1. **Production incentive plan.** Operating and maintenance employees and their supervisors are paid weekly bonuses based on the productivity of their work group. The rate is calculated based on the capabilities of the equipment employed, and no bonus is paid if the equipment is not operating. In general, the production incentive bonus can average from 80 to 150 percent of an employee's base pay.
2. **Department manager incentive plan.** Department managers earn annual incentive bonuses based primarily on the percentage of net income to dollars of assets employed for their division. These bonuses can be as much as 80 percent of a department manager's base pay.

3. **Professional and clerical bonus plan.** This bonus is paid to employees who are not on the production or department manager plan and is based on the division's net income return on assets.
4. **Senior officers incentive plan.** Nucor's senior officers do not have employment contracts. They do not participate in any pension or retirement plans. Their base salaries are set lower than what executives receive in comparable companies. The remainder of their compensation is based on Nucor's annual overall percentage of net income to stockholder's equity and is paid out in cash and stock.

Nucor seems pretty happy with the results of this approach. On July 12, 2006, the company ran the following half-page ad in *USA Today*:

How We Impressed Wall Street Without Laying Anybody Off

It seems like the easiest way to impress Wall Street these days is with massive layoffs. But we've never been accused of doing things the easy way. In fact, we've found a way to become one of the darlings of Wall Street with good old-fashioned hard work.

Rewarding that hard work with a policy of pay-for-performance. And empowering our people to make decisions for themselves. Removing red tape. Eliminating management layers. We even reward all of our employees with a program intended to send every one of their children to college. All of this resulting in not a policy, but a fact, that we've never laid off a single employee for lack of work in our entire history. Impressive even to the people on Wall Street. And they're not usually that impressed with employee retention.

FEDEX: SPOT REWARDS

In the mid 1980s, FedEx's Fred Smith asked me one day what I thought of a new spot reward program he was considering implementing. The program was known as "Bravo Zulu" and, as with many things at FedEx, emanated from the military.

According to the Department of the Navy's Naval Historical Center, Bravo Zulu is a naval signal, conveyed by flag hoist or voice radio, meaning "well done." Ships returning from a successful mission are known to hoist a Bravo

Zulu flag to signify their accomplishment. The expression has also found its way into the spoken and written vocabulary.

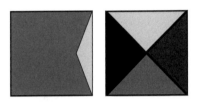

Anyhow, what he had in mind was to use the BZ symbol and expression as an instant recognition of an employee doing something well. If someone had clearly gone "above and beyond the call," any other FedEx employee (usually a manager) could recognize that effort by writing a note of appreciation upon which a BZ decal was affixed. The BZ letter could be accompanied by an award deemed appropriate by the giver—cash, tickets to an event, dinner, whatever. There were to be no—repeat, no—practical limits and no strings attached.

As has happened on more than one occasion in my life, an irreverent and acerbic tongue got the better of me as I suggested to the chairman that I didn't find this to be one of his better ideas. And, as has happened on more than one occasion, he opted not to take my advice. The program was implemented and, within weeks, it became clear to me and to the organization that it was destined to be a huge success.

I got the message personally one evening when a neighbor pulled up in her new BMW with a BZ sticker already affixed to the driver's side window, and she spent more time telling me how she earned the BZ than showing off the new set of wheels. And no, she didn't get the car as a reward, although it would have been possible. She was just so darned proud of her little BZ sticker that she wanted to show it off—especially in the FedEx parking lot.

According to the Navy, Bravo Zulu can be combined with the "negative" signal, spoken or written NEGAT, to say "NEGAT Bravo Zulu," or "not well done." A former Marine lieutenant who served two tours in Vietnam, Smith is long on military-styled acronyms and phraseology, but he has much better ways of voicing his displeasure with someone than to let them off with a simple NEGATBZ. I will likely go to my grave remembering a few of those "conversations" too.

What Mr. Smith was trying to do was create a mechanism for near real-time recognition and reinforcement of positive behavior. One needn't enact a corporate-wide program in order to exercise this principle though. Each of us can do it all by ourselves, without asking permission or going to any great expense.

DOWN 'N DIRTY

1. **Employee recognition.** Whether you use a paper calendar, Microsoft Outlook, or a PDA, put employee recognition on your "To-Do" list. Cross off the names after you've thanked or recognized each person individually.

2. **Thank-you notes.** Get some personalized thank-you notes. That's right—thank-you notes! Keep a stack of them on your desk, and a handful (with pre-stamped envelopes) in your briefcase. Whether you are at home or on a trip, take two minutes at the end of each business day to pen a note to someone who has been helpful or made a difference that day. Even if your handwriting's lousy!

3. **Drive-time thank-yous.** Use your commuting time and a cellphone (with earbud to make it safer) to leave voice mails thanking people for special effort and providing words of encouragement for someone who could use it.

CHAPTER SUMMARY

1. People will do what they are incented to do.
2. Reward and recognition measures need to be a lot more personal.
3. As Nucor has shown, pay CAN be heavily and equitably based on performance.
4. People have a basic human need to celebrate. Find meaningful ways to feed that need. Near real-time recognition and reinforcement of positive behavior can be done by anyone, without asking permission.

MONDAY MORNING, 8am

1. Initiate a conversation with your people, one at a time, to verify what their recognition preferences are, and that they are indeed being met.

CHAPTER
23

OOMPH! ON

*Wisdom is the reward you get from a lifetime of listening
when you'd have preferred to talk.*   —Doug Larson

It remains to be seen what will become of the social contract in the workplace in the years ahead; whether "the deal" continues to morph toward *Survivor*-type alliances and individualism, or the elements of loyalty, teamwork, and trust somehow get reintroduced into the mix. No one knows.

Regardless, people will still be people, complete with strengths, weaknesses, foibles, aspirations, and an incredible reserve of emotional energy they can tap into when and where they want, for reasons of their own choosing. To the degree that humans remain a vital cog in the workplace, our effort, particularly the discretionary component, will continue to matter—a lot.

For the most part, the underpinnings of motivation—the respective drivers and restrainers—will not change. People will maintain a clear preference for leaders of good character, those who reliably choose to do the right thing, even when it runs counter to their own selfish interests.

People will still want to hear the truth, even when it stings, and to be guided by those who are comfortable in their own skin. They will always want to associate with winners, understanding that the road to winning is a toll road.

They will choose optimists and be quick to follow those who can articulate in clear, compelling fashion what the journey is about and what the path forward looks like.

They will expend their discretionary capacity more liberally when the system supports and rewards (rather than frustrates) it, and when it clearly matters.

There is no guarantee that those we've come to count on as Extra Milers will continue in that vein. It is, after all, a day-by-day, moment-by-moment decision whether to Oomph! or ugh. One thing is certain—if we take it for granted, it will perish. Unfortunately, if and when that happens, we likely won't even notice until it is simply too late.

The more important issue is *you*. Will you be earning the benefit of the doubt, the benefit of the extra capacity of the people on your team? Without being overly dramatic, can you really expect to succeed and survive without it?

If you plan to see that extra Oomph!, what steps must you begin taking *now* in order to warrant its expenditure by those around you?

Should you be working on your time management, specifically that part that makes your teammates a greater priority in your life? What about your standards? Have you set the bar high enough for yourself and for those who would join you?

Is there perhaps some long-unfinished business that involves having a difficult conversation with someone in which you finally summon the courage to tell him that he must either change or leave?

Is the level of trust on your team where it should be? Is it truly at a level (a la Cirque du Soleil) where people would trust one another with their lives? Do your folks really have the discretionary authority to do their work, or are you just playing the cruel word game called "empowered"?

Do you truly care about the people on your team? How do you know you care? Do you listen, *really* listen to them? Do you make sure that no one abuses or humiliates them? Do you see to it that they don't have to pay for your mistakes? Do you care enough to tell them the truth? Do you show up when they are having a tough time?

Do you spend time daily fixing internal systemic issues so your team doesn't have to swim with an anchor? Are you fair or do you chicken out and slavishly go for consistency by hiding behind policies and the decisions of others?

Our fervent hope is that, having been reminded of the benefits and realities of this thing called discretionary effort, you will Commit—with a capital "C"—to actions that will make it a greater presence in your life. If you do, don't wait, because time is not your friend.

Good luck, Godspeed, and thank you.

ENDNOTES

SECTION 1

Chapter 1

1. Article (includes interview with Randy Moss), *Minneapolis–St. Paul Star Tribune,* November 22, 2001, www.startribune.com/stories/507/848685.html.
2. Dr. Bryan Robinson, *Chained to the Desk: A Guidebook for Workaholics, Their Partners and Children, and the Clinicians Who Treat Them* (New York: New York University Press, 2001), p. 18.
3. Interview with Command Sgt. Maj. Michele Jones, August 12, 2006.

Chapter 2

1. Russell Justice, Eastman Chemical Company, www.haygroup.com/india/ind_about.html.

Chapter 3

1. Gordon Bethune, *The Big Idea with Donny Deutsch,* January 17, 2007.
2. Ken Blanchard and Patricia Zigarmi, *Leadership and the One-Minute Manager* (New York: William Morrow & Co.), p. 50.
3. Daniel Pink, *Free Agent Nation: The Future of Working for Yourself* (New York: Warner Business Books), p. 21.
4. Tom Peters, *The Circle of Innovation: You Can't Shrink Your Way to Greatness* (New York: Vintage Books), pp. 239-240.
5. "Employee Trust and Organizational Loyalty Poll," Society for Human Resource Management and CareerJournal.com, August 2004.
6. Commerce Clearing House study, *Human Resource Executive*, December 2004, p. 46.
7. Charles Leadbetter, "The Amateur Revolution," *Fast Company Magazine,* February 2005.

Chapter 4

1. Robert Duffy, mayor, Rochester, NY, press release, City of Rochester, April 20, 2006.
2. Matthew Boyle, "The Wegman's Way" (includes interview with Sara Goggins), *Fortune*, January 24, 2005, p. 64.

SECTION 2

Chapter 5

1. Gen. Melvin Zais, U.S. Army, ret., speech before the Armed Services Staff College.
2. Rudy Giuliani, mayor, New York, Academy of Achievement interview, www.achievement.org/autodoc/page/giu0int-8.
3. Charles Hummel, "Tyranny of the Urgent" (Downers Grove, IL: Inter-Varsity Press, 1967).
4. Liz Murray, keynote address to Society for Human Resource Management convention, Washington, DC, June 25, 2006.

Chapter 6

1. Col. Ian R. Cartwright, www.au.af.mil/au/awc/awcgate/au-24/cartwright.pdf.
2. William J. Clinton, Office of the Independent Counsel Grand Jury testimony, August 17, 1998.
3. Adm. James Loy, U.S. Coast Guard, ret., "The Moral Dimension," www.uscg.mil/leadership/essays/essay2.htm.
4. Thomas J. Watson Jr., IBM, speech at Lafayette College, Easton, PA, 1964.
5. The Boy Scout Law, http://www.scouting.org/factsheets/02-503a.html.

Chapter 7

1. Gen. Melvin Zais, U.S. Army, ret., speech before the Armed Services Staff College.
2. Thomas L. Friedman, *Meet the Press*, NBC, July 30, 2006.

Chapter 8–none

Chapter 9

1. John F. Kennedy, Houston's Rice University stadium, September 12, 1962, http://www1.jsc.nasa.gov/er/seh/ricetalk.htm.

2. Terry McDermott, *Perfect Soldiers* (New York: HarperCollins, 2005), p. xvi.

3. Linda D. Kozaryn, *Defend America—U.S. Department of Defense News,* American Forces Press Service, March 14, 2002.

4. Susan C. McCraven, "Let's Roll" (includes interview with Michael Bratti), *Masonry Construction,* September 1, 2002, www.masonryconstruction.com/articles/article_template.asp?AbstractID=5976.

5. Pentagon Press briefing, from official U.S. Department of Defense transcripts, June 11, 2002.

6. http://archives.cnn.com/2002/US/09/11/ar911.memorial.pentagon.

7. Charles Garfield, *Peak Performers* (New York: Avon Books, 1986), p. 25, 80.

8. George P. Watts Jr., "What Does It Mean to be a USNA Graduate?" http://usna.com/Communities/ChapInfoCtr/Speeches/WhatItMeansToBeAGrad.htm

SECTION 3

Chapter 10

1. "Employee Engagement Report 2005," BlessingWhite, Inc., 2005.

2. "A Survey of Trust in the Workplace," DDI, 1997, www.ddiworld.com/pdf/ddi_surveyoftrustintheworkplace_es.pdf.

Chapter 11

1. American Heritage Dictionary, 4th Edition.

2. Dave Tianen, "At 79, King can still charm a crowd" (interview with B. B. King), *Milwaukee Journal Sentinel,* March 25, 2005.

3. Gen. Melvin Zais, U.S. Army, ret., speech before the Armed Services Staff College.

SECTION 4

Chapter 12

1. Thomas L. Friedman, "Let's Talk About Iraq," op-ed piece, *New York Times,* June 15, 2005, p. 23.

2. David McCullough, *1776* (New York: Simon & Schuster, 2005) p. 23.

3. Ken Olson, Digital Equipment Corporation, speech to World Future Society Convention, Boston, 1977.

4. Carlos Ghosn, Nissan Motors, speech to Foreign Correspondents Club of Japan, Tokyo, November 25, 2005.

Chapter 13
1. Andy Serwer, "The Education of Michael Dell," *Fortune,* March 7, 2005.
2. *Today Show,* NBC, May 6, 2006

Chapter 14
1. Paul B. Brown, "How Exciting" (includes interview with Joe Kraus), *Fast Company Magazine,* April 2005, p. 104.
2. James Patterson and Maxine Paetro, *The Fifth Horseman* (New York: Little, Brown, and Co., 2006), p. 214.

Chapter 15
1. Jon Wilner, "Knight's record might not last long," *San Jose Mercury News,* January 4, 2007.
2. "Knight to forgo pay after sub-par season," *Chicago Sun Times,* March 11, 2003.
3. Ibid.
4. *Brain Power,* video, Karl Albrecht International, http://karlalbrecht.com/index.htm.

Chapter 16
1. Iain Wilson, "Bank's veg row grows: cauliflower replaces cabbage," *Glasgow Herald,* August 16, 2005.

SECTION 5

Chapter 17–none

Chapter 18
1. Sarah Yost, *Gig* (New York: Three Rivers Press, 2000), p. 222.
2. "Prescriptions for Change: Delivering Bad News to Patients," *Nightline,* ABC, October 2006.
3. Ibid.

Chapter 19
1. "Global Workforce Study," Towers Perrin, 2006.
2. Ibid.

SECTION 6

Chapter 20

1. Sarah Yost, *Gig* (New York: Three Rivers Press, 2000), p. 225.

Chapter 21

1. *Brain Power,* video, Karl Albrecht International, http://karlalbrecht.com/index.htm.

2. Robert I. Sutton, PhD, *The No Asshole Rule* (New York: Warner Business Books, 2007).

Chapter 22

1. "The Maritz Poll—2005," Maritz Incentives, 2005.

2. Ibid.

3. www.nucor.com/aboutus.htm.

4. Bill Breen, "Rebel Yell" (includes interview with Matt Chambers), *Fast Company Magazine,* August 2005, p. 60.

Chapter 23–none

INDEX

231

AUTHOR BIOS

Bill Catlette is a graduate of the University of Miami School of Business. His professional background includes three decades of leadership experience in the corporate world and in his cutting-edge management consultancy. His corporate ports of call have included assignments with Genuine Parts Co. (NAPA), ADP, and FedEx. A thought leader in the field of Human Workplace Performance, he is a frequent seminar leader and keynote speaker at business meetings.

Richard Hadden has managed teams in financial services and information technology. A former software designer and university instructor, he has, since 1989, consulted with, trained, and spoken for hundreds of organizations throughout North America, Europe, and Australia. He received a management degree from Jacksonville University and an MBA from the University of North Florida. He lives with his wife and two children in his native Florida.

Contented Cow Partners, LLC

Bill and Richard founded Contented Cow Partners in 1997 to help business and organizational leaders produce better results through a focused, fired-up, and capably led workforce.

Their first book, *Contented Cows Give Better Milk*, published in 1998, is based on the premise, supported by their research, that creating a great place to work is one of the best things any organization can do for its bottom line. It has been widely acclaimed by businesspeople and educators worldwide as an authoritative source that makes the business case for being an employer of choice.

The firm consults with and conducts leadership training for companies and other organizations around the world. Bill and Richard are popular keynote speakers at corporate/ association meetings and conferences.

HOW TO CONTACT US

For booking information
http://www.contentedcows.com/booking

To order books
http://www.contentedcows.com/orderbooks

To receive our leadership newsletter, *Fresh Milk*
http://www.contentedcows.com/freshmilk

For more information about us
http://www.contentedcows.com/information

Contact Bill
Phone: 901.853.9646 or E-mail: Bill@ContentedCows.com

Contact Richard
Phone: 904.720.0870 or E-mail: Richard@ContentedCows.com